TREVOR WYE &
PATRICIA MORRIS

PRACTICE BOOK
for the *Piccolo*

Novello Publishing Limited
14-15 Berners Street, London W1T 3LJ

Exclusive distributors:
Music Sales Limited
Newmarket Road
Bury St. Edmunds
Suffolk IP33 3YB.

Order No. NOV120658
ISBN 0-85360-137-2
This book © Copyright 1988 Novello & Company Limited.

ALSO AVAILABLE

The Piccolo Study Book NOV120829

Practice Book for the Flute Volume 1 Tone NOV120510

Practice Book for the Flute Volume 2 Technique NOV120522

Practice Book for the Flute Volume 3 Articulation NOV120523

Practice Book for the Flute Volume 4 Intonation & Vibrato NOV120550

Practice Book for the Flute Volume 5 Breathing & Scales NOV120588

Practice Book for the Flute Volume 6 Advanced Practice NOV120591

Practice Book for the Flute Omnibus Edition Books 1-5 NOV120851

Proper Flute Playing NOV120651

The Orchestral Flute Practice Book 1 NOV120801

The Orchestral Flute Practice Book 2 NOV120802

The Alto Flute Practice Book NOV120781

CONTENTS

		Page
	PREFACE	4
	INTRODUCTION	5
Section A	*Middle register:* Tone and Intonation	6
	Loud playing	12
	Low register: Tone	14
	Daily practice	17
	Intonation and Tone colour	17
	Intonation	17
	Cork position	17
	Tone colour	18
	Vibrato	18
Section B	*Articulation*	47
	Low register	50
	General articulation	51
	Single tonguing	51
	Double tonguing	53
	Triple tonguing	57
	Some odd ones	58
	Flutter tonguing	64
	Repeated notes	77
Section C	*Tunes at the top*	84
	Loud playing	84
	Quiet playing	88
	Nuances in general	90
	Smoothing out the bumps	91
Section D	*Special Fingerings*	103
Section E	*Some well-known tunes to play*	105
	Grace-notes	105
Section F	*Notes to look at*	126
	Harmonic fingerings	127
	Tchaik. 4	134
Section G	*Piccolo Duets*	185
Section H	*Coda*	193
	A work-out routine	193
	Auditions	197
	A list of very probable audition pieces	197
	Buying a piccolo	197
	Further repertoire	198
	A list of chamber works containing piccolo	199
	A list of piccolo solos	201
	INDEX	203
	ACKNOWLEDGEMENTS	209

PREFACE

Here, we believe, for the first time is a comprehensive Practice Book for the Piccolo. Well, almost complete but for one ingredient; the work you, the reader, must put in.

The recipe is as before. It's all a question of *time, patience* and *intelligent work,* plus another ingredient, courage.

This book is designed to help the flute player transfer his playing techniques to the piccolo, to view the piccolo as an extension of the flute, and to understand the adjustments to be made when changing from one instrument to the other.

To become familiar with the piccolo and its eccentricities, it makes sense to use the orchestral repertoire. It is, after all, first and foremost, an orchestral instrument. It has many possible colours to add to the orchestral texture, but is not widely written for as a solo instrument.

Although it cannot contain all the passages written for the piccolo this book does provide the opportunity to obtain a good working knowledge of the frequently used orchestral repertoire, and of some less familiar pieces. It will also provide a good practice schedule enabling you to deal with the various building blocks of piccolo technique as shown by the section headings. We thought it helpful to organise the book in this way to enable you to contemplate some of the problems. There is a full listing in the index on page 203.

If you are inexperienced on the piccolo, start at the beginning and work your way through the book.

INTRODUCTION
The Flute Versus the Piccolo: Differences

The piccolo is an extension of the top register of the flute. The lower and middle registers of the piccolo should be thought of as the middle and upper registers of the flute respectively.

Yes, breath support and embouchure are different for the piccolo but not *very* different. In whatever way you play the flute, everything is more compact on the piccolo.

The blow hole is smaller and the breath support greater.

When we first try an alto, or even a bass flute, the first few minutes are usually frustrating because we try to play it in the same way as the more familiar concert flute. To obtain a real tone on these instruments, we discover that the embouchure has to be more relaxed, especially for the low register. In fact we discover that the nicest, roundest sound is obtained by the minimum lip pressure and a larger hole is required between the lips.

The reverse is true of the piccolo; the hole needs to be smaller. To meet this need the lips will have to be trained with exercises.

Remember Practice Book 1 – TONE* – for the flute; 'increase the air speed when ascending'? The air speed should increase by yet another factor to produce a beautiful tone on the piccolo, especially in the third octave.

Making a start

You are anxious to make a start, but before plunging into the deep end, observe these few guidelines; they will, in time, help you to make quicker progress.

* It is unwise to start off your day on the piccolo like a demented banshee. Do some flute practice first to warm the lips.
* Practise the third octave of the flute each day before your piccolo practice. Take note of the extra air speed and of how you 'hold' the smaller hole in your lips without undue tension.
* If, or when your lips feel strained and tired, then stop. Don't squeeze the notes out.
* Each day will be different. When progressing from the second to the third octave, should you feel tense or strained then stop. Don't try to focus the tone too quickly. In athletics, you would run only as fast as you reasonably can; to overdo it would result in a pulled muscle. It's the same with the lips.
* If you have a wide flute vibrato, cut it down on the piccolo unless you want to sound hysterical. Use enough vibrato to keep the tone alive. Try to keep your vibrato *within your tone*. Refer to Practice Book 4 – INTONATION – in the section on Vibrato.
* Whenever possible, refer to a recording of the appropriate passage for piccolo to capture the mood of the piece. Some excerpts contain very few notes and could be dismissed as too easy for serious practice. Wrong! These seemingly sparse bits can be your downfall in the real orchestral situation.
* Metronome marks are given as a guide only as conductors vary in their interpretation of speeds. The speeds quoted are those most most commonly used in orchestras today.
* Finally be conscious of intonation. It must be the central focus of all that you practise. Whatever you achieve on the piccolo *it must be in tune*.

*a TREVOR WYE Practice Book for the Flute, Volumes 1-6 (Novello)

SECTION A

Middle Register: Tone and Intonation

TONE

Our first aim will be to make the piccolo an extension of the flute; to be equally flexible and as expressive as the flute.

A common problem is the shooting upwards of Right Hand middle register notes like E which is inclined to split.

Much of this problem is due to (a) improper placing of the piccolo on the lip or (b) covering too much of the blow hole with the lower lip; (c) air stream problems: you need less air but more abdominal support than for the lower and middle registers of the flute.

On the flute, the lip plate is placed lower than for the piccolo: due to its size, you will have to experiment using your ears, and a mirror to obtain the optimum position for the piccolo which will have to be higher on the bottom lip than for the flute. Your experience, and previous tone exercises will help you find the right spot.

Practise these exercises to find out where the best placing is, and to discover exactly where these notes are:

Keep your throat open and relaxed to avoid restricting the air stream in this part of the register; the control is from the abdominal muscles. Remember, intonation is very important at this stage: carelessness now will mean unlearning what you have already accomplished.

Intonation is a central issue on the piccolo.

Now practise Exercise 3 to obtain a singing quality to your tone.

Take it easy with your lips: don't overwork them. All the intervals should sound without strain.

When this exercise can be played easily, go on to:

Now you are ready to try the following pieces:

ENIGMA VARIATIONS
Variation VIII

ELGAR

MOTHER GOOSE SUITE
II Petit Poulet

RAVEL

SYMPHONY No. 2
4th Movt. – Finale

TCHAIKOVSKY

ST ANTHONY VARIATIONS
Variation VIII·

BRAHMS

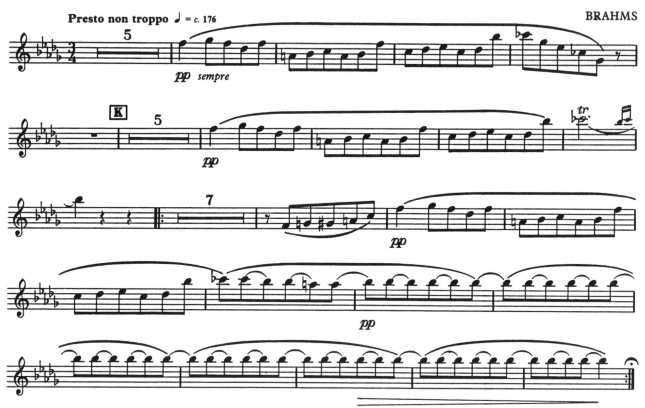

*It is advisable to practise these last 12 bars with a metronome in order to maintain the tempo as well as the pitch and diminuendo!

SLAVONIC DANCES
Op. 46 No. 1

DVOŘÁK

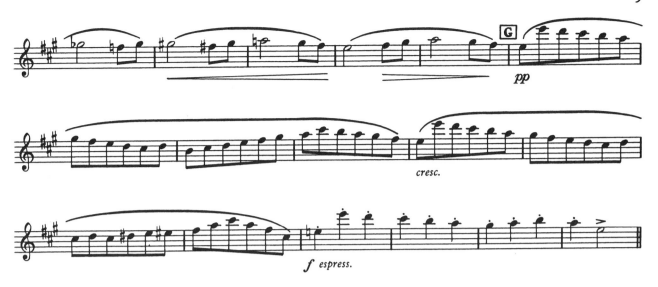

THE FIREBIRD

STRAVINSKY

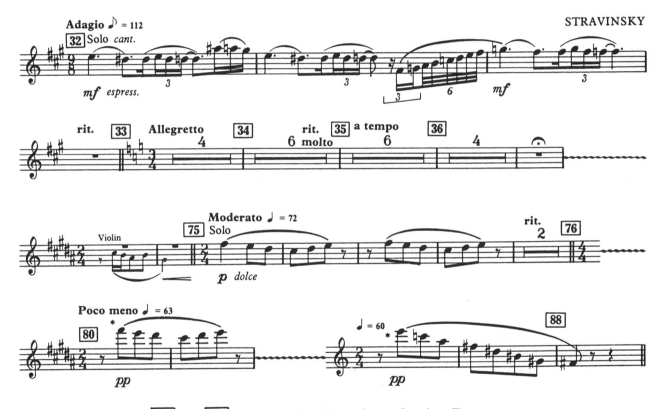

*For advice on fig. 80 to 88, see Special Fingerings, Section D.

3rd Movt.

SCHEHERAZADE
1st Movt.

RIMSKY-KORSAKOV

ROUMANIAN DANCES
III Pe Loc

BARTÓK

LOUD PLAYING

You will be required to play very loudly sometimes in the middle and low registers. Practise these exercises to help you crescendo and so obtain a full sound.

As you ascend, do not push yet more air through; it only makes it more difficult for the lips to cope. *Do*, however, keep the air speed and increase the breath support.

Take special care to keep your throat free as you ascend, and make sure that the upper notes do not sound louder or brighter than the rest.

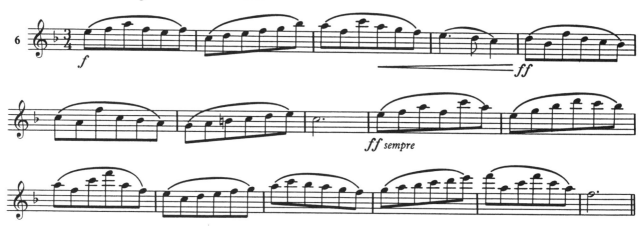

Then try the following tunes:

RITE OF SPRING
Adoration of the earth

STRAVINSKY

SYMPHONY No. 5
4th Movt.

BEETHOVEN

LOW REGISTER: TONE

The low register of the piccolo has been described as sounding like a dove with asthma.
We must correct this impression. The low register is sometimes used for an unusual orchestral tone colour and sometimes, too, for comic effect.
Practise these exercises:

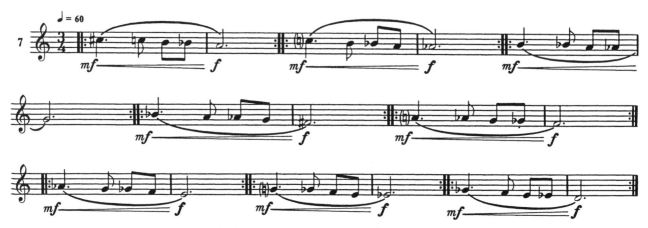

Turn now to Practice Book 1 – TONE*, page 11 and practise Exercise (b), (c) and (d). And now turn to the Verdi Requiem extract and practise with an expressive and full tone.

REQUIEM
No. 1 Requiem

VERDI

Repeat a tone lower (E min.), a third lower (D min.) and then a fifth lower (B min.).
Practise now the following pieces keeping the colour constant throughout the range.

THE PERFECT FOOL

HOLST

*Novello & Co. Ltd.

SYMPHONY No. 4
3rd Movt.

BRAHMS

MOTHER GOOSE SUITE
III Laideronnette, Impératrice des Pagodes

RAVEL

This section needs to be practised *mf* in order to cut through the orchestral texture.

From Fig. 19, it is much easier if you leave the F♯ key down all the time.

IV Les entretiens de la Belle et de la Bête

LA MER
II Jeux de Vagues

DEBUSSY

DAILY PRACTICE
Every Day: Practise the first six exercises in this book as a warm-up then turn to Practice Book 1 – TONE*, pages 16 and 17 and practise Exercises 10, 11 and 12.
Baroque Sonatas are also excellent practice at this stage.
It would be advantageous to look at Section H – Advice on buying a piccolo, now.

Now practise Debussy *Jeux* and Dvořák *Symphony No. 6* taking very special care of intonation.

JEUX

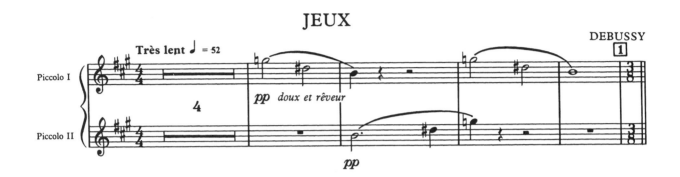

SYMPHONY No. 6
3rd Movt.

INTONATION AND TONE COLOUR
Intonation is possibly the most nerve-wracking feature of playing the instrument in the orchestra. It is often placed at the top of the chord in a hideously prominent position, and there are anxious moments sitting on top of the ladder others have built. The piccolo chair usually receives the brickbats and often with some justification.

INTONATION
Unfortunately, the scale of the piccolo, that is, the tone hole placements, do not seem to have been regularised. Instruments vary a great deal. Many older instruments have flat G's and A's and middle D and D♯ tend to be sharp in some modern instruments.
The conical piccolo bore generally flares out at the foot for the last inch or so. Filling in this flare with plasticene will generally flatten D and D♯ and give a more regular scale.
Read pages 15 and 17 in Practice Book 4 – INTONATION – for general advice on these problems.

CORK POSITION
This doesn't follow the usual rules as for the flute (see Practice Book 4, page 17 paragraph 4). The best placement for the cork in conical piccolos seems to be quite near the embouchure hole. As the headjoint bore is 11 mm., the cork should start off 11 mm. from the *centre* of the mouth hole. Make a mark 11 mm. from the end of a cleaning stick and place the cork first in that position. From this starting point, it will be used to be pushed in. Some players find that 9 mm. is good, others even less: check the tone, then check both the A♮ and the octaves.

*Novello & Co. Ltd.

If you are having difficulties with the top register push the cork in a bit; it will probably help but make sure you haven't weakened the lower octave too much.

Because the piccolo has such small proportions and a small blow hole with a small aperture between the lips, any adjustments have a correspondingly greater effect on the pitch.

In order to obtain some flexibility in pitch, practise 'bending' notes as in Practice Book 1, page 34. Practise the exercise at the bottom of the page. DO THAT FIRST.

Now practise the exercises on page 35, Nos. 2 and 3. Then practise the glissando in Berlioz: *Symphonie Fantastique*, 3 bars after fig. 60, page 35.

Finally, turn to Practice Book 4, page 25 – 24 studies for intonation. Vary the nuances. Change the printed expression marks. Practise Nos. 2, 3, 4, 6, 8, 9, 13, 15, 20 and 21 an octave higher. Observe the idiosyncrasies of your instrument as you play the octaves, fifths and thirds.

TONE COLOUR

You will find that in the orchestra, the problems of intonation vary with the tone colour of the accompanying instrument. For example there is no room for error when playing in unison or octaves with the clarinet (as in R. Strauss: *Don Juan*) or oboe, but it is generally more comfortable with bassoon or flute. Violins are better but not when they are playing harmonics as in Ravel: *Mother Goose*. The glockenspiel is always a problem as it is usually a long way across the orchestra and intonation problems are inaudible to you – but not the audience, i.e. Arnold: *English Dances*. It will be found useful to be able to change the colour to make the sound wider and less well defined and focussed as in the 'Aquarium' exercise in Practice Book 1. This will lessen the harmonic content and reduce the likelihood of intonation clashes.

It is necessary to have enough flexibility in pitch to cope with all the problems you are likely to meet. That means practice.

VIBRATO

As we pointed out in the Introduction, vibrato should be *inside* the tone; try to contain it within the tone you have. As it develops, your vibrato may have to be modified. So do it.

Read the section on vibrato in Practice Book 4, page 19 and join in at any stage you think might be helpful.

If your vibrato is fine on the flute, it will be too wide on the piccolo. As the violin is to the cello, so the piccolo is to the lower octave of the flute. Piccolo vibrato will need to be faster and shallower. If there are already problems with your flute playing such as too wide a vibrato, or worse, an aged nanny-goat vibrato, then these will cause added problems on the piccolo. They should be corrected first.

You may feel impatient and want to get on with piccolo playing but your success on the 'little flute' will only be as great as its weakest part. Correcting your vibrato will also enhance your flute playing; after all, the piccolo is an added extension of the flute.

So, do it now.

Now you are ready to practise the remaining pieces in this section.

Back to the Flute

As this is a Piccolo Practice Book for flute players, it's a good idea to maintain one's flute playing after a bout with the 'little flute'.

This will help to take any stiffness out of the lips. Flexibility exercises can be found in many volumes of studies and in Practice Book 1 for the Flute.

You will also find whistle-tone practice on both the flute and the piccolo, very helpful in relaxing the lips.

SYMPHONY No. 8
4th Movt.

SHOSTAKOVICH

The metronome helps you to check the evenness of the quintuplets and the ties.

5th Movt.

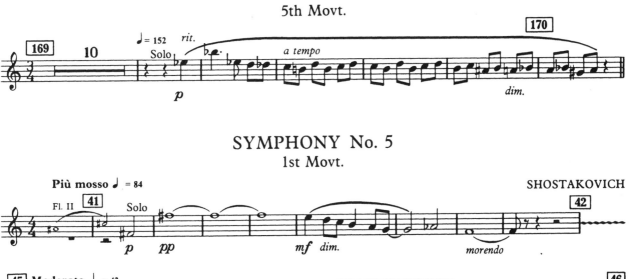

SYMPHONY No. 5
1st Movt.

SHOSTAKOVICH

SYMPHONY No. 6
1st Movt.

SHOSTAKOVICH

*For help with F♯, see Special Fingering, Section D.

SYMPHONY No. 9
2nd Movt.

SHOSTAKOVICH

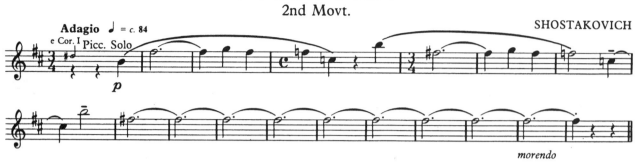

SYMPHONY No. 8
2nd Movt.

SHOSTAKOVICH

Page 21

CHANT DU ROSSIGNOL

STRAVINSKY

CAUCASIAN SKETCHES
No. 4 Cortège of the Sardar

IPPOLITOV-IVANOV

*Special fingering for G♯s – see Section D.

SCHEHERAZADE
3rd Movt.

Andantino quasi Allegretto ♩. = 63

RIMSKY-KORSAKOV

SYMPHONY No. 9
(from the New World)
1st Movt.

♩ = 136

DVOŘÁK

Horn (sounding an octave lower)

Picc. Solo

TURKISH MARCH

BEETHOVEN

Vivace ♩ = 126

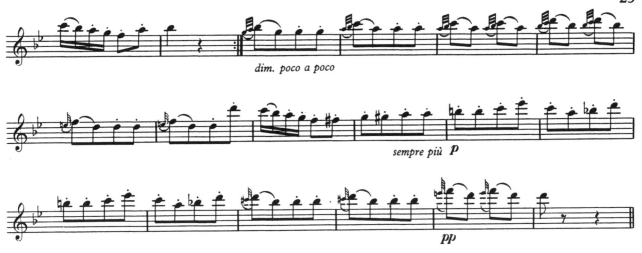

dim. poco a poco

sempre più **p**

pp

OVERTURE - IL SERAGLIO

MOZART

THE SONG OF THE EARTH
3rd Movt.

MAHLER

4th Movt.

THE FOUNTAINS OF ROME

La fontana di Valle Giulia all'alba

RESPIGHI

La fontana di Villa Medici al Tramonto

SYMPHONY No. 7
2nd Movt.

MAHLER

HORN CONCERTO
2nd Movt.

HINDEMITH

NOBILISSIMA VISIONE
2nd Movt. - March & Pastorale

HINDEMITH

SYMPHONY No. 1
1st Movt.

MAHLER

REQUIEM
No. 2

BRAHMS

No. 6

PIANO CONCERTO No. 2
1st Movt.

BRAHMS

4th Movt.

ST ANTHONY VARIATIONS
Variation V

BRAHMS

SERENADE
Opus 16
Rondo

BRAHMS

DIVERSIONS FOR THE LEFT HAND
Variation VI – Nocturne

Andante piacevole ♩. = *c.* 63

BRITTEN

VIOLIN CONCERTO No. 1
1st Movt.

PROKOFIEV

2nd Movt.

Some extracts are very short. You may wonder why they have been included. Under orchestral performing conditions, these short and seemingly harmless fragments can be difficult; you may not have the chance to warm up before. So, practise them. You only have *one* chance to come in, on the beat, expressively and in tune!

3rd Movt.

OVERTURE – ROMAN CARNIVAL

BERLIOZ

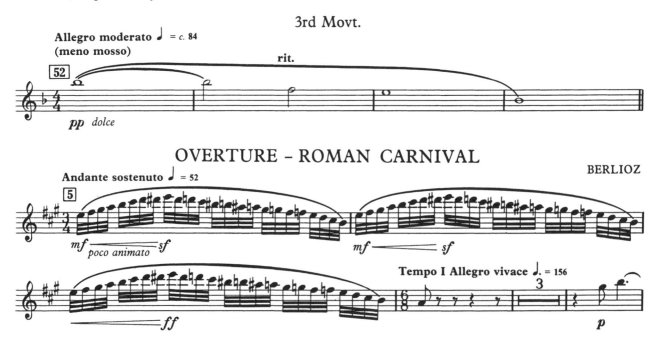

34

SYMPHONY No. 1
2nd Movt.

SHOSTAKOVICH

SYMPHONY No. 15
4th Movt.

SHOSTAKOVICH

Practise also the 2nd piccolo part of Shostakovich's 10th Symphony, 1st Movt., on page 185, Section G.

SYMPHONIE FANTASTIQUE
2nd Movt.

BERLIOZ

5th Movt.
A Witches' Sabbath

POLOTSVIAN DANCES

BORODIN

OVERTURE – BEATRICE AND BENEDICT

BERLIOZ

SYMPHONY No. 5
3rd Movt.

CONCERTO FOR ORCHESTRA
3rd Movt. – Elegia

4th Movt. – Intermezzo interrotto

5th Movt.

SCHWANDA THE BAGPIPER
Polka

WEINBERGER

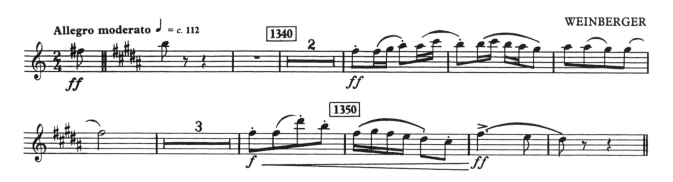

Fugue

SLAVONIC DANCES
Op. 46 No. 2

DVOŘÁK

No. 3

DANCES OF GALANTA

KODALY

41

ENGLISH DANCES SET I
No. 1

ARNOLD

No. 3

ENGLISH DANCES SET II
No. 5

ARNOLD

No. 6

No. 7

FOUR SCOTTISH DANCES

No. 2

ARNOLD

No. 3

SYMPHONY No. 2
1st Movt.

TCHAIKOVSKY

SYMPHONY No. 2
3rd Movt.

MAHLER

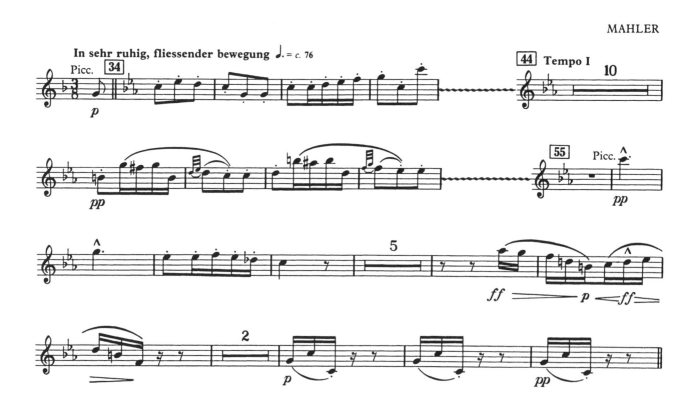

SYMPHONY No. 5
4th Movt.

SHOSTAKOVICH

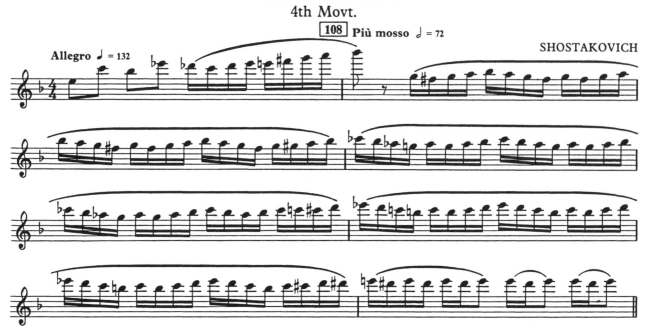

L'ENFANT ET LES SORTILEGES

RAVEL

SECTION B
Articulation

In matters of articulation, we assume you are already proficient in single, double and triple tonguing. If you are not, then we would refer you to Practice Book 3 – Articulation (Revised version 1983) particularly the exercises on page 10. Articulation must have bounce.

When you have achieved these techniques, they are readily transferable to the piccolo.

They will be particularly effective if you have worked at allowing the tongue to interfere as little as possible with the air stream. This is most important as your articulation can sound very clumsy on the piccolo for reasons stated before – everything is reduced in size on the piccolo, and that means the movement of the tongue should be very light, the tip of the tongue travelling the minimum distance and thereby causing the least disturbance in the mouth.

Articulation exercises are tone exercises and good articulation is useless if the tone is of poor quality. When using the tongue, the beginner often moves the *whole* tongue. This can be seen in a mirror when there is a lot of movement in the throat. One of the aims of the exercises is to transfer the action to the front of the tongue *only*. This takes time.

Here are some passages which require a clean articulation in the low register. Start with the Ravel Piano Concerto and practise legato first, that is, slurred, to obtain a clear tone. Keep a strong air stream upon which to articulate.

Then practise the Rossini and Dvořák.

PIANO CONCERTO
1st Movt.

RAVEL

OVERTURE – THE SILKEN LADDER

ROSSINI

SLAVONIC DANCES
Op. 46 No. 2

DVOŘÁK

Practise *Peter Grimes* next; don't use TE–KE as the clearest result will be obtained by TE–DE and will make the *first* of each pair stronger than the second. Avoid taking a breath between each pair.

SEA INTERLUDES
from 'Peter Grimes'
Sunday Morning

BRITTEN

Now practise the remainder in this Group.

THE SORCERER'S APPRENTICE

DUKAS

Make sure there are no noises reminiscent of bacon sizzling on the D or the F.

REQUIEM
No. 7 Libera me

VERDI

SYMPHONY No. 4
2nd Movt.

MAHLER

Be careful of the pitch of the octave Gs.

50

LOW REGISTER

Piccolo – low C: Billy Budd (Britten)

It must be annoying to come across this little piece when you've bought a good piccolo but it won't play low C and D flat. There's no way around it except borrowing or hiring one, or one could, at a pinch, play it on a treble flute in G. The conductor just might not notice!

BILLY BUDD
Act II – Scene 3

BRITTEN

GENERAL ARTICULATION

SINGLE TONGUING

One special form of single tonguing should be practised at this point; it is the articulation produced with the tongue between the lips as described in Practice Book 6, page 26.

Be sure to practise it *carefully*; this form of articulation is most often misunderstood.

The exercises, involving tonguing between the lips, produce 'dew-drop' notes as in *William Tell*, *The Force of Destiny*, and mixed in with other articulations as in the *Faust Ballet Music*, and in Tchaikovsky's *6th Symphony*. The first movt. has been included here, but need not be practised yet. To be able to produce this 'dew-drop' quality is an important adjunct to the orchestral player. First practise these exercises followed by the passages mentioned above.

OVERTURE – WILLIAM TELL

ROSSINI

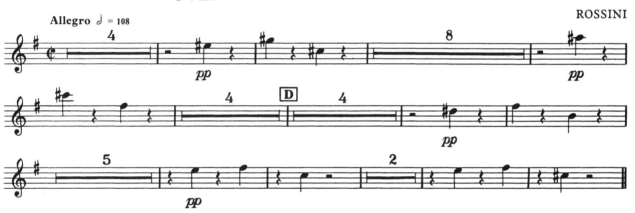

OVERTURE – THE FORCE OF DESTINY

VERDI

BALLET MUSIC – FAUST
Section D

GOUNOD

SYMPHONY No. 6
1st Movt.

TCHAIKOVSKY

3rd Movt.

DOUBLE TONGUING
It is helpful to practise DE–GE rather than TE–KE as this may help keep the articulation clearer and less percussive, a problem for exposed solos when the movement of the tongue inside the mouth can sometimes be heard.
Practise the following passages.

OVERTURE – DI BALLO

SULLIVAN

THE VALKYRIE
Wotan's Farewell and Fire Music

WAGNER

55

REQUIEM
No. 3 Offertorio

No. 4 Sanctus

No. 6 Lux aeterna

BALLET MUSIC – FAUST
Section C

GOUNOD

TRIPLE TONGUING

It is worth practising DE-GE-DE-GE-DE-GE instead of the usual DE-GE-DE, DE-GE-DE in fast tempi, as the latter has a tendency to break up the groups into separate triplets i.e.:

This distorts the rhythm and causes anxiety amongst the rest of the woodwind! When the tempo is very fast, it becomes a necessity to use DE-GE-DE, GE-DE-GE; the avoidance of two successive 'DE-DES' facilitating the speed. Start by practising *Daphnis and Chloe* (Part I) on page 78, starting with DE-GE-DE, DE-GE-DE. Then practise DE-GE-DE, *GE-DE-GE*; become fluent in both ways. Similarly, practise *Chant du Rossignol* and *La Mer* below.

CHANT DU ROSSIGNOL

STRAVINSKY

LA MER
II – Jeux de vagues

DEBUSSY

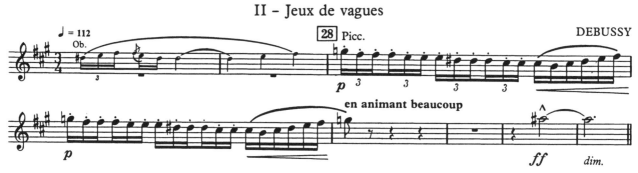

Some Odd Ones:

A Practise the following exercise using the articulation indicated:

Now using the same articulation, move on to *Prince Igor, Scheherazade, Billy the Kid*, and *Faust Ballet Music* (see page 52).

OVERTURE – PRINCE IGOR

BORODIN

SCHEHERAZADE
4th Movt.

RIMSKY-KORSAKOV

BILLY THE KID

COPLAND

B Practise carefully, *Chant du Rossignol*. The articulation was written in by the composer. This has puzzled many players. The most likely explanation is that he thought, at that time, that, like flutter tonguing, it was a special effect.

CHANT DU ROSSIGNOL

STRAVINSKY

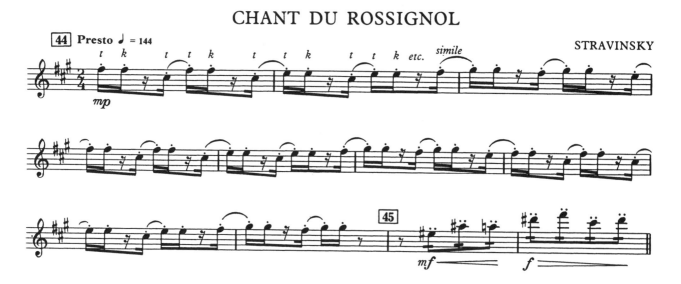

YOUNG PERSON'S GUIDE TO THE ORCHESTRA
Fugue

BRITTEN

C Young Person's Guide; the problem here is the necessity to be flexible enough to play softly *immediately* after the indicated accents. It can be practised a number of ways; first, all slurred, and observing the nuances when tongued. Then try these:

and then:

finally, the whole solo.

D This rhythm often appears:

and should be practised with the articulation indicated and the correct note lengths as follows:

This allows you to practise the correct rhythm in *Scheherazade* – even at great speed.

SCHEHERAZADE
2nd Movt.

RIMSKY-KORSAKOV

E For these articulations: the difficulty lies in the repeated notes. Do not shorten the last note of the slur and make sure they remain even semiquavers.

In the case of the second example you must practise both articulations – DE–GE DE–GE becomes essential at speed.

Practise Volume 3 – Articulation – page 15, Exercise 18, and page 14, Exercises 12 and 13, using these articulations. Then go on to the following extracts, being especially careful to accurately place the note after the rest of ♪ ♫♫. Breathe in the previous bar and resist the temptation to breathe on the downbeat.

OVERTURE - THE JOURNEY TO RHEIMS

ROSSINI

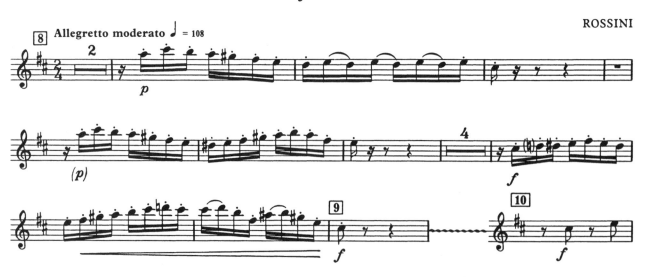

OVERTURE – THE BARBER OF SEVILLE

ROSSINI

LA MER

II – Jeux de vagues

DEBUSSY

LE COQ D'OR
Cortège des noces

RIMSKY-KORSAKOV

Now turn to Stravinsky's *Firebird Suite*, 3rd Movt., Section A, page 9, which has the same articulation.

FLUTTER TONGUING

It's sometimes called for in the repertoire.

There are two ways of producing it:

(a) the tongue loosely flaps in the air stream and (b) throat flutter.

Most people find that one or the other works for them; which you choose is only important as far as it affects the lips. A flutter which causes movement at the embouchure opening disturbs the tone and makes it difficult to play both in the low and high octaves.

Find out which is easiest; then find *any* note on which it is most effective and which disturbs the lips the least. From that note slowly descend chromatically and stop when the tone becomes weak. Repeat and try to extend the range.

This method is just as effective on the flute where one is often required to flutter down to low C. To flutter in the top, again find your best and easiest note and slowly ascend whilst fluttering. Pianissimo flutter is the hardest and to prevent the first part of the note from exploding, *tense the abdominal muscles first*: don't do it at the moment when you have to play – it's too late then! Remember the tongue cannot flutter without the air stream.

If you have practised all the previous exercises, you should have little difficulty with the remainder of this section.

SCHEHERAZADE
2nd Movt.

RIMSKY-KORSAKOV

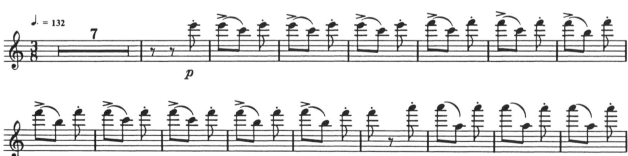

Last Movt.

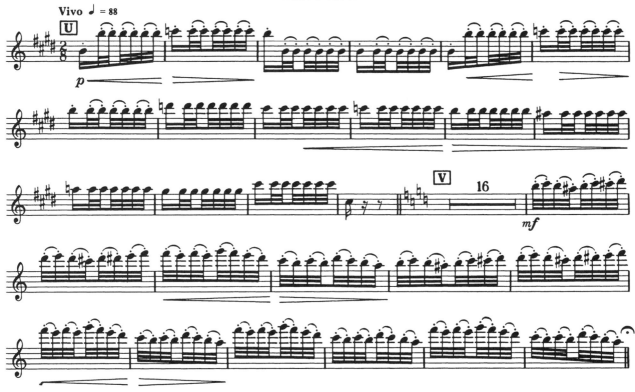

OVERTURE – WILLIAM TELL

ROSSINI

BILLY THE KID
Scene 1a
Street in a frontier town

COPLAND

The open prairie

GOLDEN AGE
2nd Movt.

SHOSTAKOVICH

DIVERSIONS FOR THE LEFT HAND
Variation IXb – Toccata II

BRITTEN

DANCE OF THE COMEDIANS

SMETANA

DANCES OF MAROSSZEK

KODALY

IPHIGENIA IN TAURIS
Act I Chorus

GLUCK

Rinaldo: as it stands, this extract looks as though every note is tongued. Unless you have an 'edited' version, the wise piccolo player will place some slurs in to blunt the otherwise frantic effect of the solo. A conductor will often indicate what he wants, so be prepared for anything, but we have made a suggestion indicated by dotted lines.

RINALDO
Aria and Cadenza, Scene VI

HANDEL

70

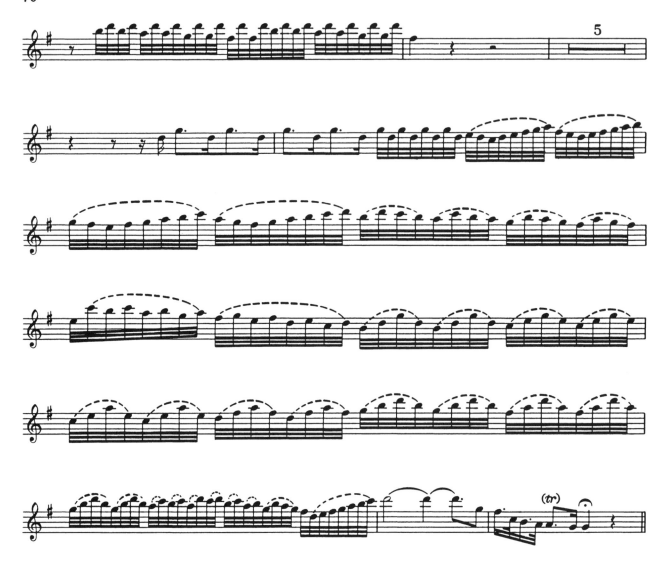

RHAPSODIE ESPAGNOL
4th Movt. Feria

RAVEL

OVERTURE – SEMIRAMIDE

ROSSINI

SYMPHONY No. 2
4th Movt.

TCHAIKOVSKY

EIN HELDENLEBEN

R. STRAUSS

OVERTURE – SICILIAN VESPERS

VERDI

JEUX D'ENFANTS
Galop

BIZET

DANCES OF GALANTA

KODALY

LA CALINDA

DELIUS

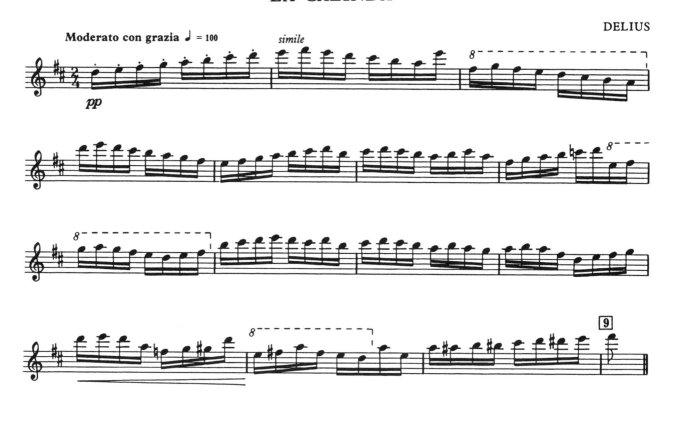

BALLET MUSIC – FAUST
Section G

GOUNOD

OVERTURE - THE SIEGE OF CORINTH

Repeated Notes

ROSSINI

Repeated notes can cause rhythmic problems in scale passages. The clue in the passage above lies in the accent and in the D—GE D—GE articulation practised previously.

DAPHNIS and CHLOE
Part I

RAVEL

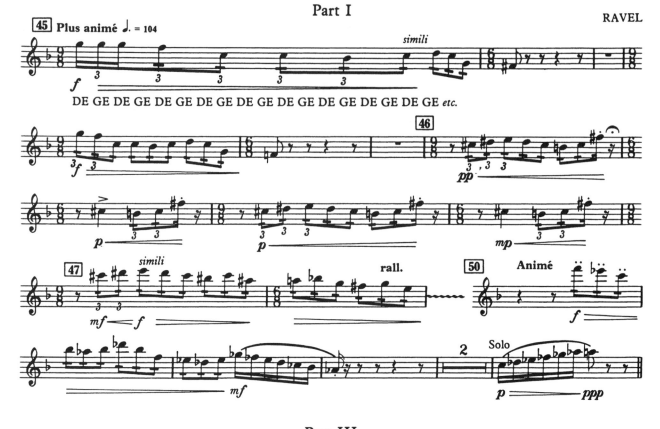

DE GE DE GE DE GE DE GE DE GE DE GE DE GE DE GE DE GE *etc.*

Part III

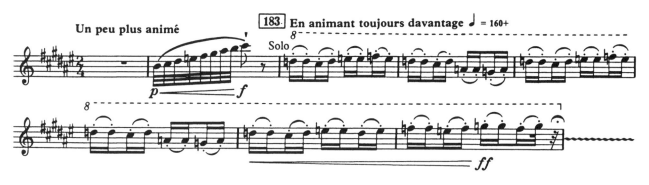

L'ARLESIENNE SUITE I
Pastorale

BIZET

Farandole

AIDA
Finale

VERDI

SYMPHONY No. 15
1st Movt.

SHOSTAKOVICH

SYMPHONY No. 9
1st Movt.

SHOSTAKOVICH

COPPELIA
No. 11 Musique des automates

(A)

DELIBES

The second extract from Coppelia is similar to the first (fig. 67) but at the double bar, continue straight on to Section B without stopping. It's good practice.

(B)

No. 2

Allegro ♩ = c. 120

No. 3

Allegretto non troppo

84

SECTION C
Tunes at the top

LOUD PLAYING

Sometimes, you are required to play very loudly. This can be an endurance test for you, your cats, and your neighbours. We suggest you use cotton wool earplugs to increase your endurance, particularly as *difference tones* (see Practice Book 4) can interfere with your hearing.

First, practise the Expressive Scales and Arpeggios as set out in Practice Book 5 – Breathing and Scales – in order to obtain freedom in obtaining the notes, and observe the following points.

(a) Don't try to play quickly; keep it loud but not sharp.
(b) Choose the scales which take you *gradually* into the top register.
(c) Play naturally; don't back off when ascending.
(d) Stop frequently on the way up, and 'bend' notes as set out previously.
(e) Pay attention to the evenness of nuances when ascending.
(f) If the top is insecure, unsafe or just loud *and* coarse, then practise the middle register first. It can vary from day to day.
(g) Carefully monitor how much air you need to maintain the same dynamic tone. There is a tendency to use too much air as you ascend and this can be a painful experience! It can also be counter productive because sudden bursts of extra air force the hole in your lips to open, and puts a greater strain on the muscles.

Now repeat these expressive scales and arpeggios *mf*.

On your first good day, try the following extracts.

OVERTURE – WILLIAM TELL

ROSSINI

NOBILISSIMA VISIONE
2nd Movt. – March & Pastorale

HINDEMITH

See also Berlioz *Roman Carnival Overture* in Section A from fig. 19, page 33.

SYMPHONY No. 5
2nd Movt.

SHOSTAKOVICH

This is to check your stamina!　　　4th Movt.

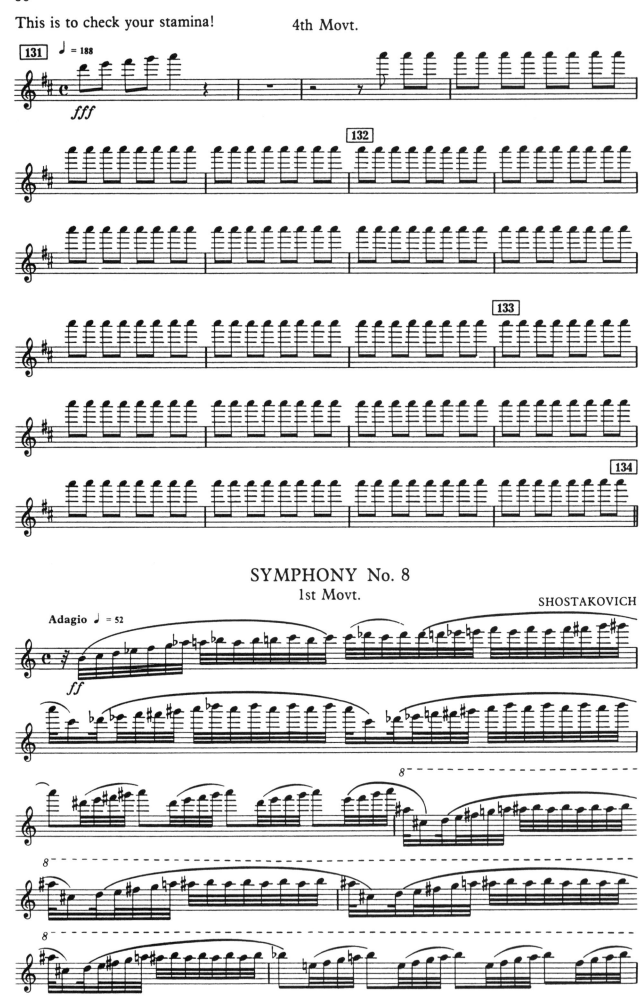

SYMPHONY No. 8
1st Movt.

SHOSTAKOVICH

SYMPHONY No. 8
2nd Movt.

SHOSTAKOVICH

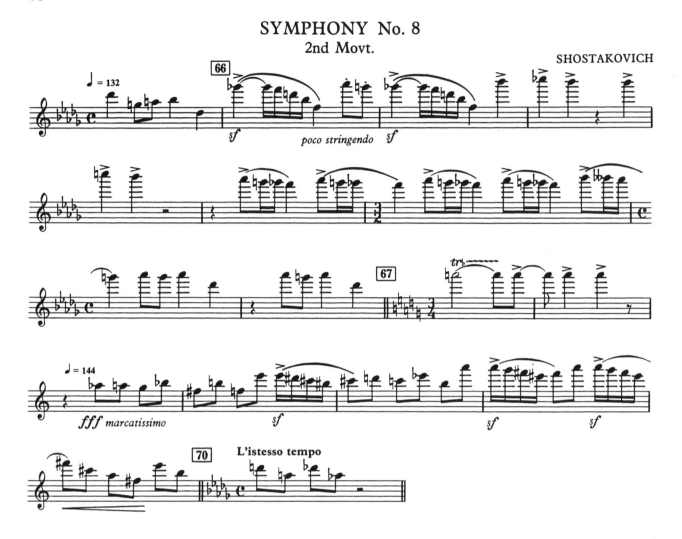

QUIET PLAYING

On other occasions you will need to play very quietly. To help you gain this facility, practise this exercise on the flute to help you gain the correct embouchure for the piccolo. The small blowing hole thus gained without too much tension, and the direction of the air stream is very useful in playing *pp* at the top of the piccolo.

Now, take up the piccolo and try these experiments:

(a) with the lips closed, finger top E, and blow with enough air speed to part the lips. Blow no harder than the absolute minimum to achieve that note. As you become expert in the direction, and amount of air needed, you will be able to continue up the scale to at least B flat.

(b) finger top E but blow straight ahead and not into the hole so that there is *no sound* whatever. Use the correct air speed *as if you are going to play top E*. You'll have to pretend. Now gradually lower the thin pencil of air until it *just touches* the opposite edge of the hole and hold it there.

Repeat.

Use the right air speed; do not rely on a great *quantity* of air to produce the speed.

Both these experiments will give you an insight into how to properly control the tone and nuances at the top end of the piccolo. (See also Practice Book 6, p.27.)
Now practise Beethoven's *9th Symphony*, the section before and after letter I with a little shimmer of vibrato. Keep the expressive quality constant as you ascend.

SYMPHONY No. 9
Last Movt.

BEETHOVEN

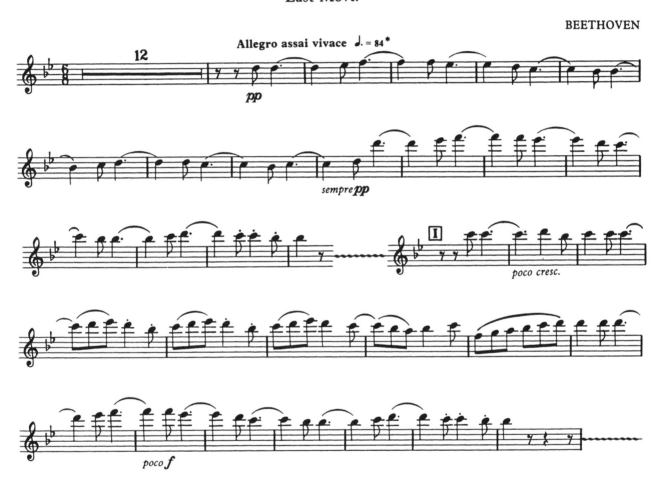

Now see if you can extend your dynamic range throughout the whole section up to letter K.

*In spite of Beethoven's given speed, this is usually played at ♩.= 104-126.

NUANCES IN GENERAL

You may notice that the piccolo sounds louder as you ascend; this is, in part, due to the change in colour.

Try to avoid this change of colour and it will at least help to create the illusion of playing quietly.

Try to keep some *breadth* in the sound; spread it rather than centre it.

Practise these exercises. Listen to the quality of the sound whilst ascending: try to keep it the same. The top should be no brighter than the middle.

Next practise Ravel's *Bolero*, Section H, page 190, Stravinsky's *Firebird*, Section A, page 9 and Ravel's *Rhapsodie Espagnol* below.

Don't make the sound too incisive but as shaded, and as *ppp* as possible.

RHAPSODIE ESPAGNOL
2nd Movt. - Malaguena

RAVEL

SMOOTHING OUT THE BUMPS

This next excerpt we can use as a study for continuity from the low to the top octave though it is a complete and continuous extract. First, try line two; practise *f*, *mf* and *pp*. Remember what you have previously learned in this section: (a) air speed, (b) don't back off: play naturally, and (c) keep the expression constant.

THE FOUNTAINS OF ROME
La fontana di Trevi al Meriggio

RESPIGHI

Now practise lines 3, 5, 4 and 1 in that order; use the 'long' fingering for top G sharp – i.e. *add* 3rd & 4th fingers of R.H.

Continue your practice with the remainder in this section.

SYMPHONY No. 11
2nd Movt.

SHOSTAKOVICH

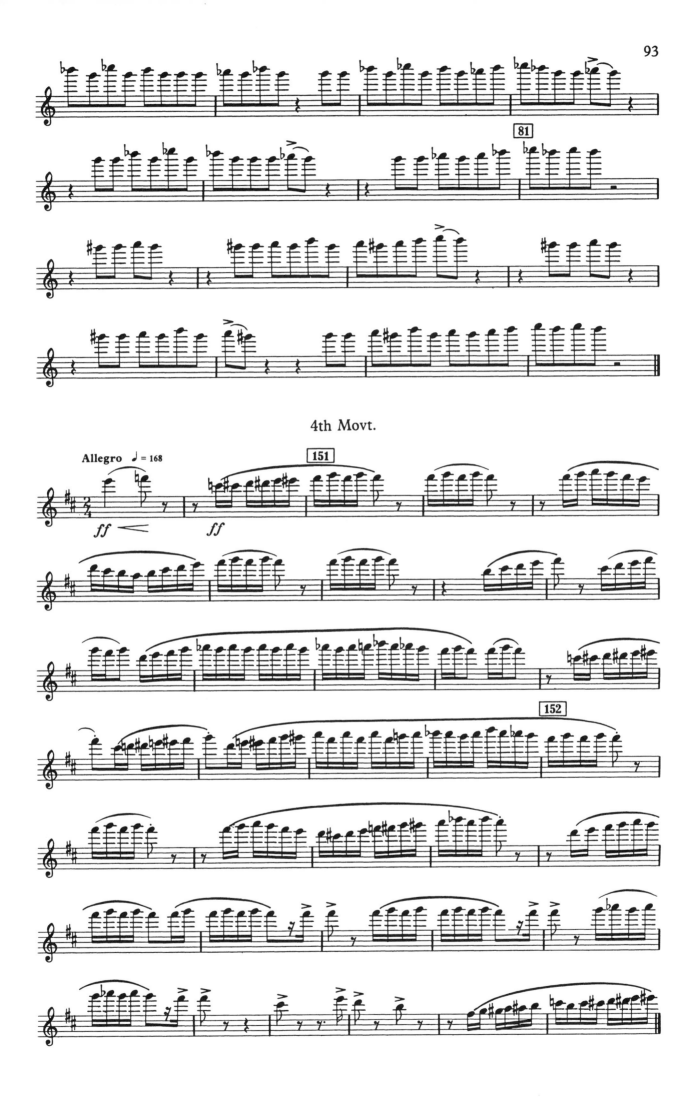

4th Movt.

94

SYMPHONY No. 12
1st Movt.

SHOSTAKOVICH

4th Movt.

SYMPHONY No. 13
1st Movt.

SHOSTAKOVICH

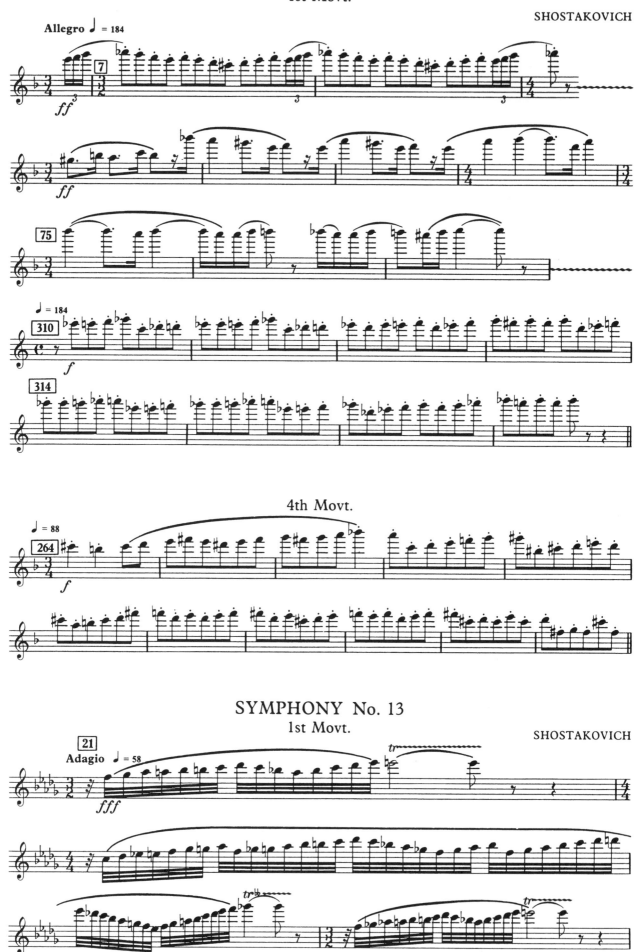

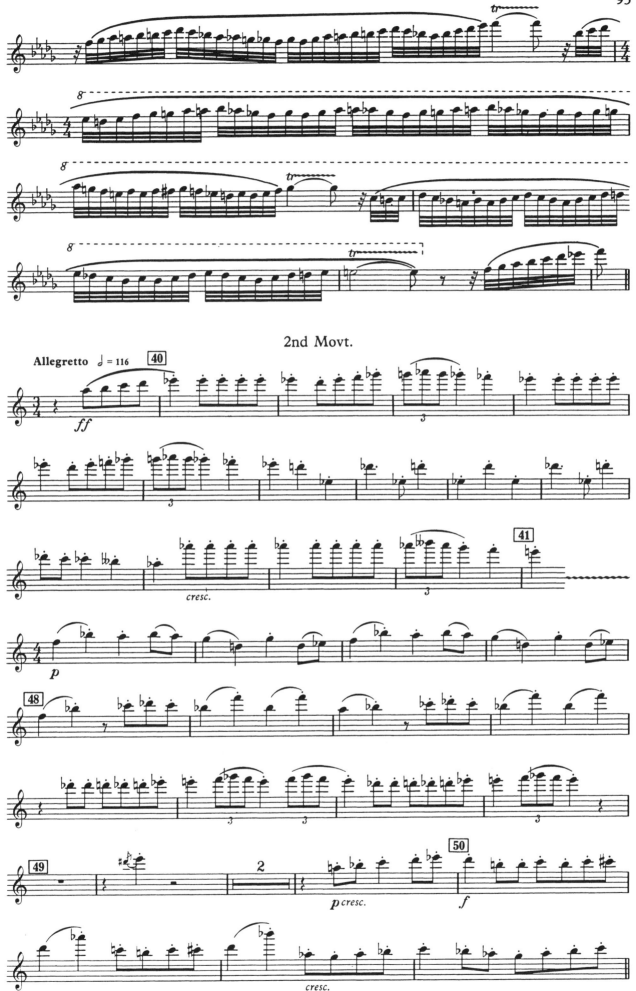

2nd Movt.

5th Movt.

SYMPHONY No. 15
4th Movt.

SHOSTAKOVICH

OVERTURE – THE BARTERED BRIDE

SMETANA

97

DANCE OF THE COMEDIANS

SMETANA

98

POLKA

SMETANA

FURIANT

SMETANA

HARY JANOS SUITE
II – Viennese Musical Clock

KODALY

VI – Entrance of the Emperor and his Court

100

(VI – Entrance of the Emperor and his Court)

CONCERTO FOR ORCHESTRA

KODALY

See also Stravinsky *Firebird Suite*, Section A, page 9; Rimsky-Korsakov *Scheherazade*, Section B, pages 62, 64; Dvořák *Slavonic Dances, No. 2*, Section A, page 39.

OVERTURE – ROMAN CARNIVAL
(also in Section A)

BERLIOZ

SYMPHONY No. 7
1st Movt.

MAHLER

THE LOVE OF THREE ORANGES
2nd Movt.

PROKOFIEV

SECTION D
Special Fingerings

It really would be useless simply to try these fingerings out, and exclaim 'ooh! *that* one's good!' *Unless you have incorporated these fingerings into your daily practice, at a moment of stress you will forget them.* And that will be the very moment when you *most* need them.

So, try them by all means; then practise some scales and arpeggios so that they become second nature to you. The first five fingerings will enable you to start the note *ppp*; there is less resistance and it's very much sharper. Top G sharp (6) nearly always needs to be fingered using the 'long' fingering, to avoid the 'kick' in it.

No. 7 is a sharper B flat. On many instruments, though there may be a healthy C, there may be no top B. If you have problems, try No. 8.

For when you blow 'fiftissimo', here are some flatter fingerings, Nos. 9, 10 and 11.

When playing middle A, B flat and B *piano* with diminuendo, it's useful to use the G sharp key to sharpen the pitch.

Use the 'long' fingering for top G sharp in the *Karelia* extract below.

KARELIA SUITE
III Alla marcia

SIBELIUS

Hansel and Gretel is an example of the useful pianissimo C, both at Q and in the last three bars.

OVERTURE – HANSEL and GRETEL

HUMPERDINCK

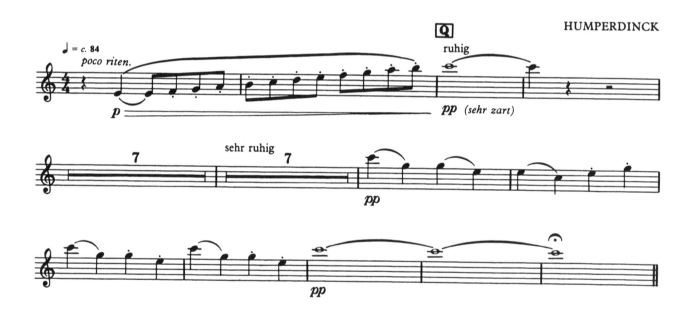

See also Stravinsky's *Firebird Suite*, Section A, fig. 80 to 88 , page 9, for the first E and F sharp.

SECTION E
Some well-known tunes to play

GRACE-NOTES

This section is up to you. But, there is something often required on the piccolo which is an important adjunct to have: the short, crushed grace-note.

Practise this until the short note is almost non-existent; the long note being really long.

The next bit is to be practised until the small note is entirely crushed against the quaver, or quarter note, and has *almost no value whatever*, but is clearly audible.

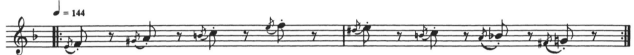

This exercise should sound rather like a dripping tap. You will often encounter this brilliant writing in piccolo music.

Now look at the *Young Person's Guide*, and the *Symphonie Fantastique*.

YOUNG PERSON'S GUIDE TO THE ORCHESTRA
Flutes' Variation

BRITTEN

SYMPHONIE FANTASTIQUE
5th Movt. – A Witches' Sabbath

This needs to be played with the first finger B flat lever key.

BERLIOZ

And now on to the rest of this section.

OVERTURE – SEMIRAMIDE

ROSSINI

SYMPHONY No. 2
1st Movt.

BORODIN

FINALE

LIEUTENANT KIJE

PROKOFIEV

107

SYMPHONY No. 3
3rd Movt.

DVOŘÁK

CAPRICCIO ESPAGNOL
III Alborado

RIMSKY-KORSAKOV

110

IV Scena e Canto Gitano

V Fandango Asturiano

OVERTURE - ABU HASSAN

WEBER

OVERTURE – THE MERRY WIVES OF WINDSOR

NICOLAI

SCHERZO CAPRICCIOSO

JEWELS OF THE MADONNA SUITE
III Serenata

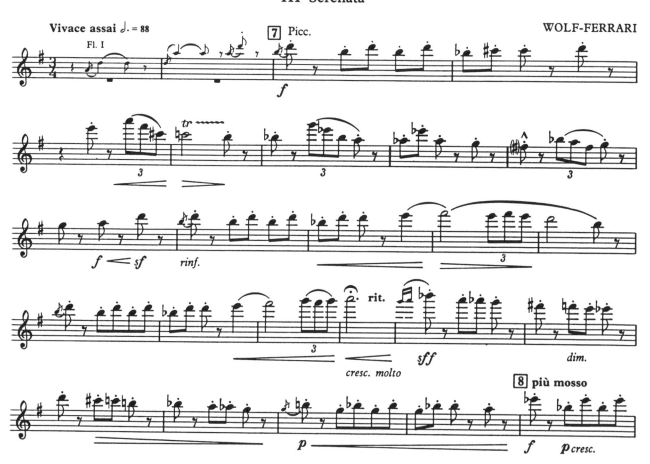

IV Danza Napolitana

114

NORTH AMERICAN SQUARE-DANCE SUITE
Introduction

BENJAMIN

No. 1 Miller's Reel

LE COQ D'OR
Introduction

RIMSKY-KORSAKOV

FAÇADE SUITE I
Polka

WALTON

3 Swiss Yodelling Song

4 Tango Pasadoble

5 Tarantella Sevillana

THE NUTCRACKER SUITE
Chinese Dance

TCHAIKOVSKY

OVERTURE – THE THIEVING MAGPIE

ROSSINI

118

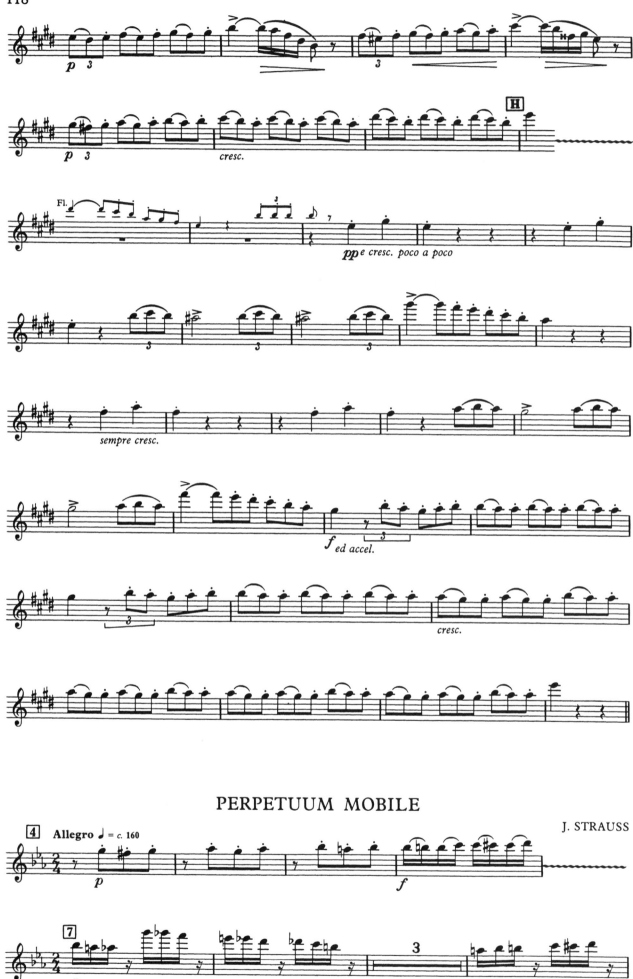

PERPETUUM MOBILE

J. STRAUSS

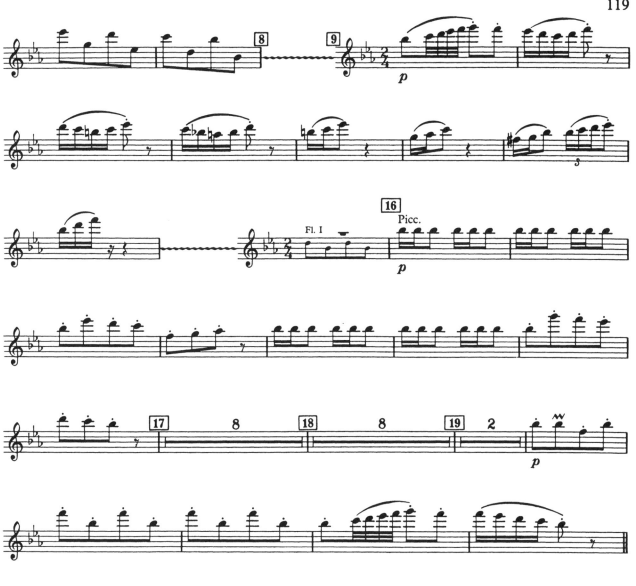

OVERTURE – EGMONT

BEETHOVEN

VARIATIONS ON A NURSERY TUNE
Variation IV

DOHNÁNYI

Allegretto moderato ♩ = *c.* 126

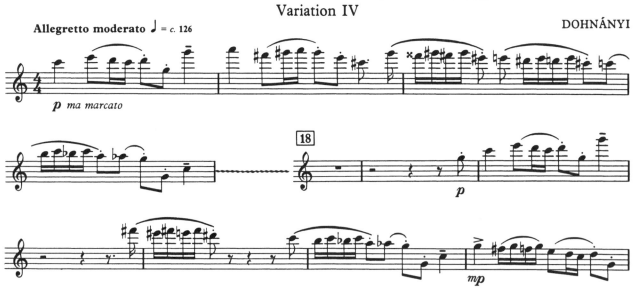

LA CALINDA

DELIUS

THE LOVE OF THREE ORANGES
3rd Movt. – Marche

PROKOFIEV

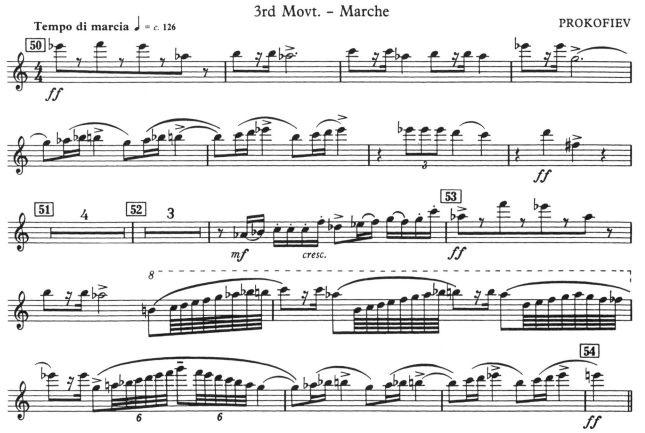

PIANO CONCERTO No. 2
1st Movt.

SHOSTAKOVICH

3rd Movt.

VARIATIONS ON A THEME OF PAGANINI
Variation XIII

RACHMANINOV

[Variation XIV]

SYMPHONY No. 7 (LENINGRAD)
1st Movt.

SHOSTAKOVICH

SYMPHONY No. 9
3rd Movt.

SHOSTAKOVICH

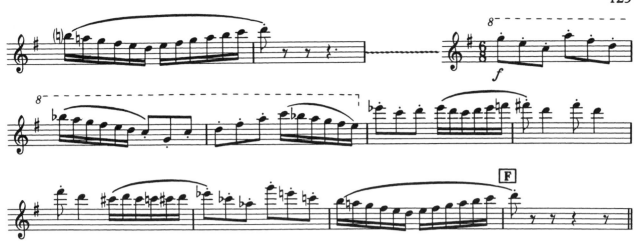

5th Movt.

CARMEN SUITE
1st Movt.

BIZET

*repeat 8va and **pp***

SECTION F
Notes to look at

This section fills in the gaps in the repertoire. We have included them because it would be more comfortable to have had a preview than to have to sight-read followed by frantic practice!

In matters of fingers, your flute technique should be readily transferable to the piccolo, even though it feels different. The balance of the keys is different than on the flute. Try it out on a study you have learnt, say one of the Andersen Opus 15 or a Drouet study or simply practise the Daily Exercises in Practice Book 2 but starting on D.

Then have a go at the Verdi Requiem – *Libera me*. Iron out the irregularities in evenness by short and frequent bouts of technical practice.

REQUIEM
No. 7 Libera me

VERDI

HARMONIC FINGERINGS

Some pieces – with some conductors – go so fast that we have to resort to the use of the trill keys and harmonic fingerings, for it is our only hope. But, of course, this cannot be a last-minute decision. You must learn them at least as thoroughly as your normal fingerings so that they are always available in an emergency.

This short exercise will amply repay the time spent learning the fingerings and will give you a choice of F sharps depending on the notes around it. When the notes and fingerings are familiar, play the exercise very quickly.

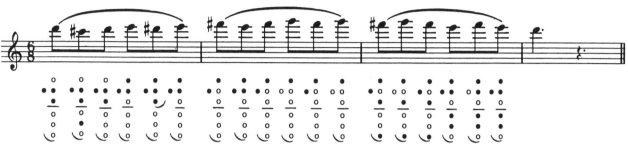

Three more exercises, together giving a choice of fingerings. Players, and instruments vary; when you have practised them, the choice will be yours.

Don't feel that you are cheating; fingering charts are academic up to a point. Beyond that, the whole idea is to play the music accurately and neatly.

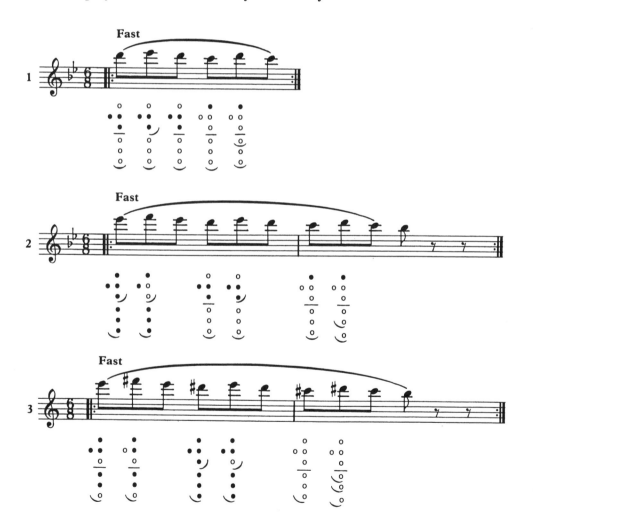

Also, work at the two following extracts. The letters T and H suggest passages where trill or harmonic fingerings should be practised.

OVERTURE – BEATRICE AND BENEDICT

BERLIOZ

For the main notes, e.g. E flat, D and C in bars 3 and 4, use the regular fingering, trill fingerings for the interim notes.

POLOTSVIAN DANCES

BORODIN

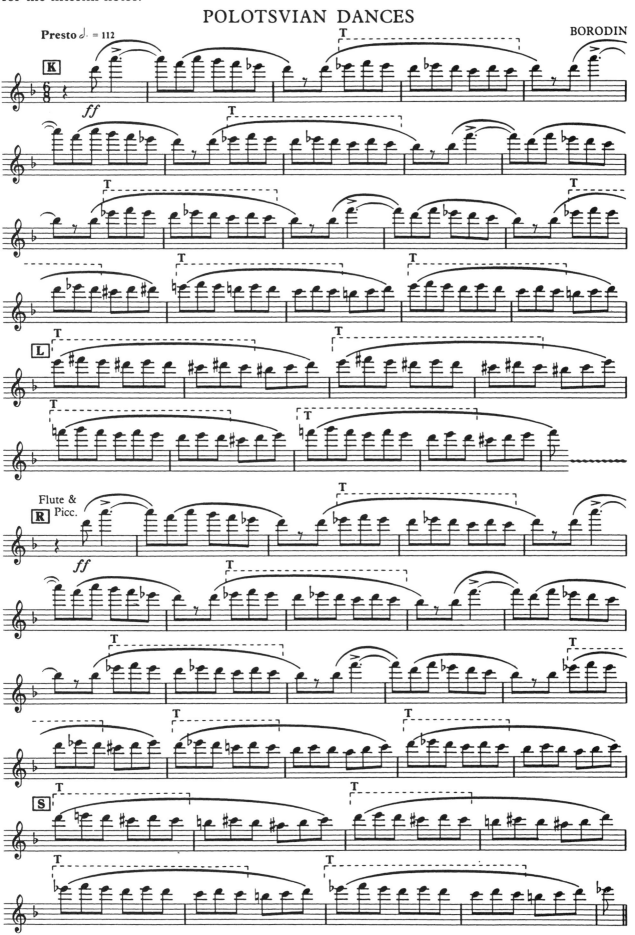

The rest of this section is now up to you!

WOZZECK

BERG

In the passage above ⌐ indicates a solo or important thematic material.   Γ indicates a less important passage.   ⌐ indicates the end of an indicated passage.

HARY JANOS SUITE
I PRELUDE – THE FAIRY TALE BEGINS

KODALY

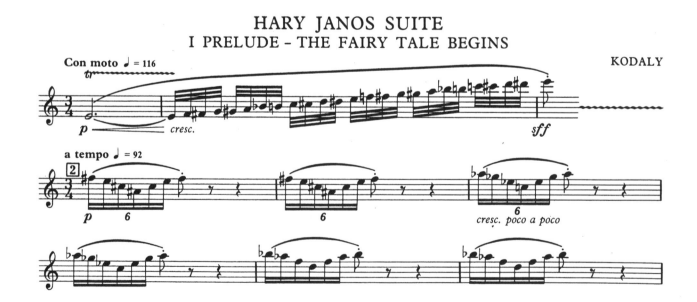

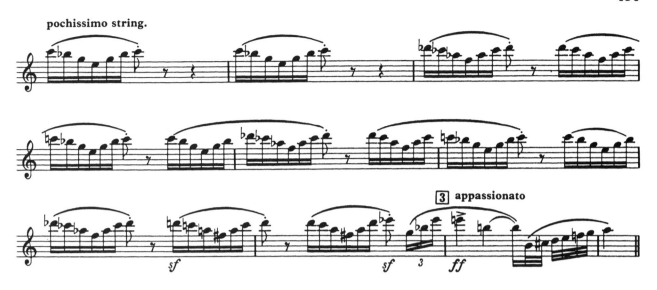

A bit in the Kodaly *Dances of Marosszek* you should know about: at fig. 132, the next four bars are played in the time of four beats. We have indicated where the beats are. First learn the notes, then set your metronome to ♪ = 150 (4 × 150 ♪ = 600; 6 × 100 ♪ = 600).
Practise the passage with four beats to a bar. At the ⁴⁄₈, return to ♪ = 100.

DANCES OF MAROSSZEK

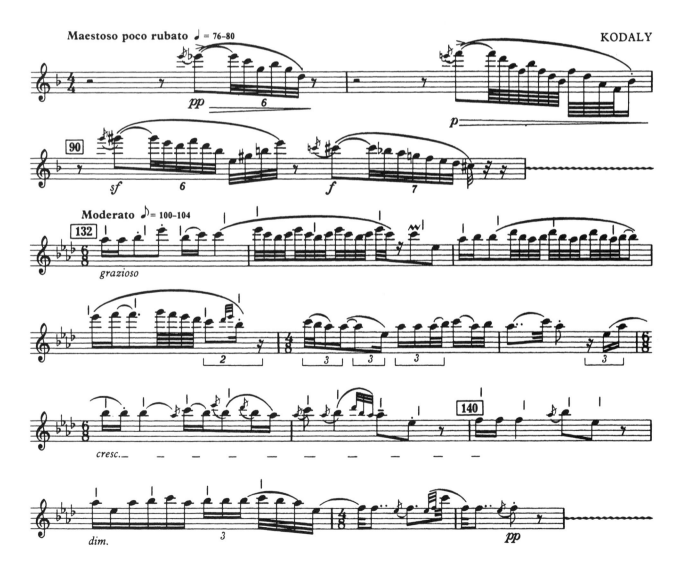

SYMPHONY No. 5
1st Movt.

NIELSEN

TCHAIK. 4

The piccolo repertoire abounds in short-lived teasers amongst which is the famous Tchaikovsky 4th Symphony passage:

Here is an exercise which you can also use for many other tricky corners. Practise it first legato. Check the evenness of both fingers and tone. Keep the support constant; no sudden bursts of air for the top E flat or A flat.

Practise it in the following ways:

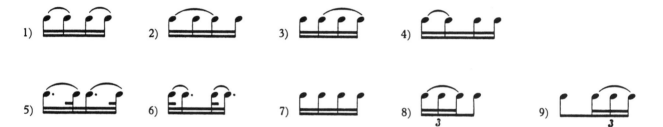

Maintain constant support and keep your throat relaxed.

Now practise this, being careful to place the C natural exactly on the second quaver beat of the 2nd bar.

Now you need to practise the whole passage in G, A, B flat and B major. Don't write it out unless you *really* have to. It would be better to memorise it.

SYMPHONY No. 4
3rd Movt.

TCHAIKOVSKY

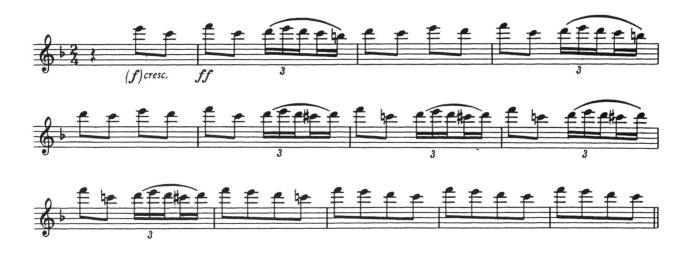

4th Movt.

CONCERTO FOR ORCHESTRA
5th Movt.

BARTÓK

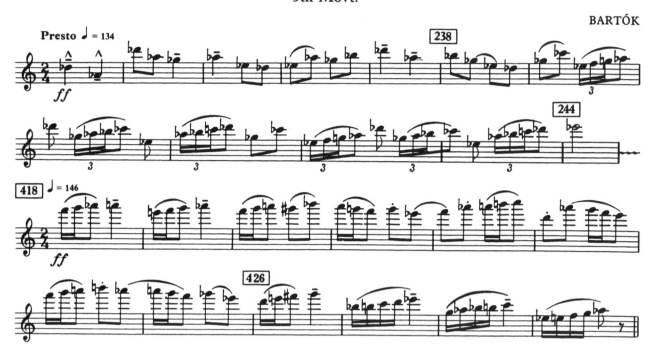

THE FIREBIRD
L'Oiseau de feu et sa danse

STRAVINSKY

Note: The excerpt here is from *The Firebird* complete ballet. The equivalent solo in *The Firebird* Suite is significantly different. As that version is more frequently required at auditions than this one, the Suite version is printed on page 211.

138

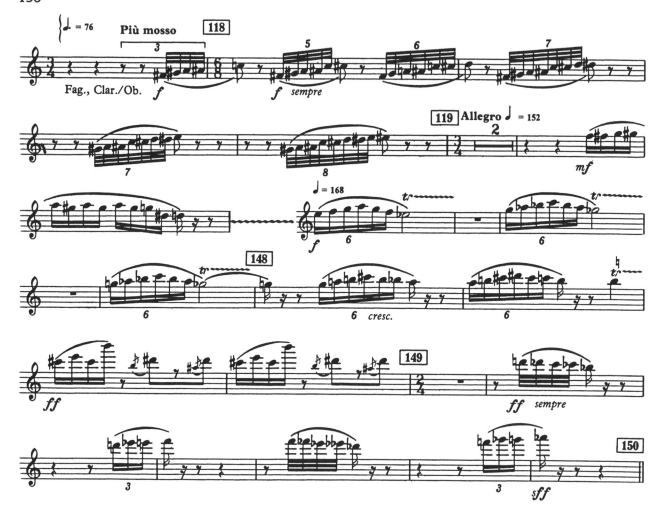

BALLET - THE SLEEPING BEAUTY
Canari qui chante

TCHAIKOVSKY

SINFONIETTA
3rd Movt.

JANÁČEK

RITE OF SPRING
Adoration of the earth

STRAVINSKY

Dance of the adolescents

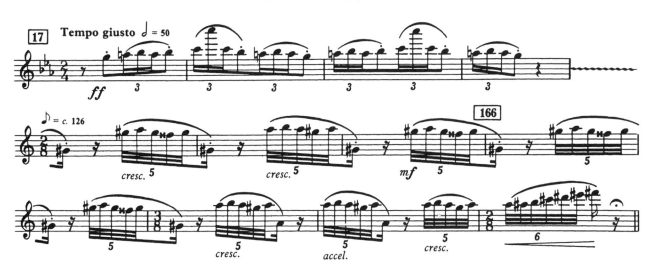

OVERTURE – SCAPINO

WALTON

MANFRED SYMPHONY
1st Movt.

TCHAIKOVSKY

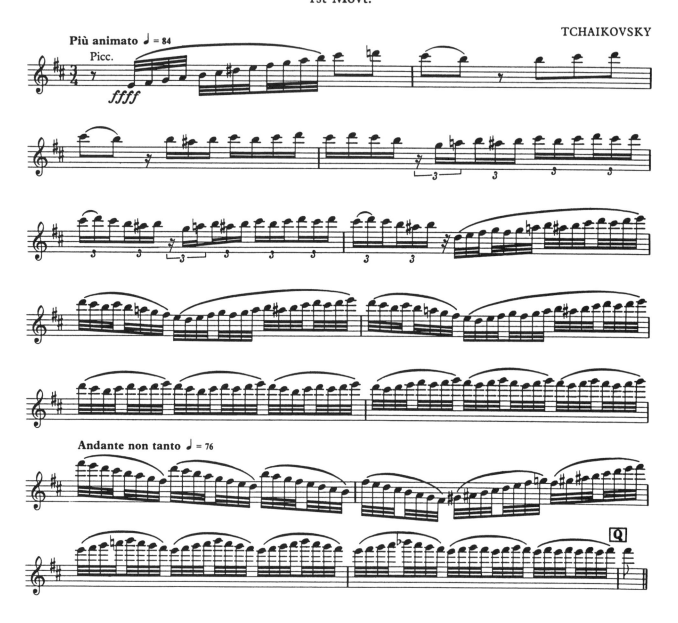

4th Movt.

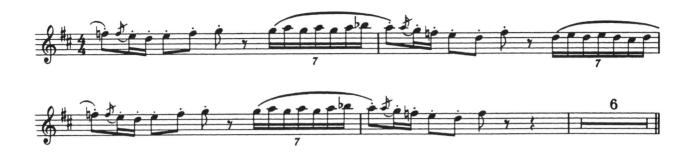

TILL EULENSPIEGEL

R. STRAUSS

THE SORCERER'S APPRENTICE

DUKAS

144

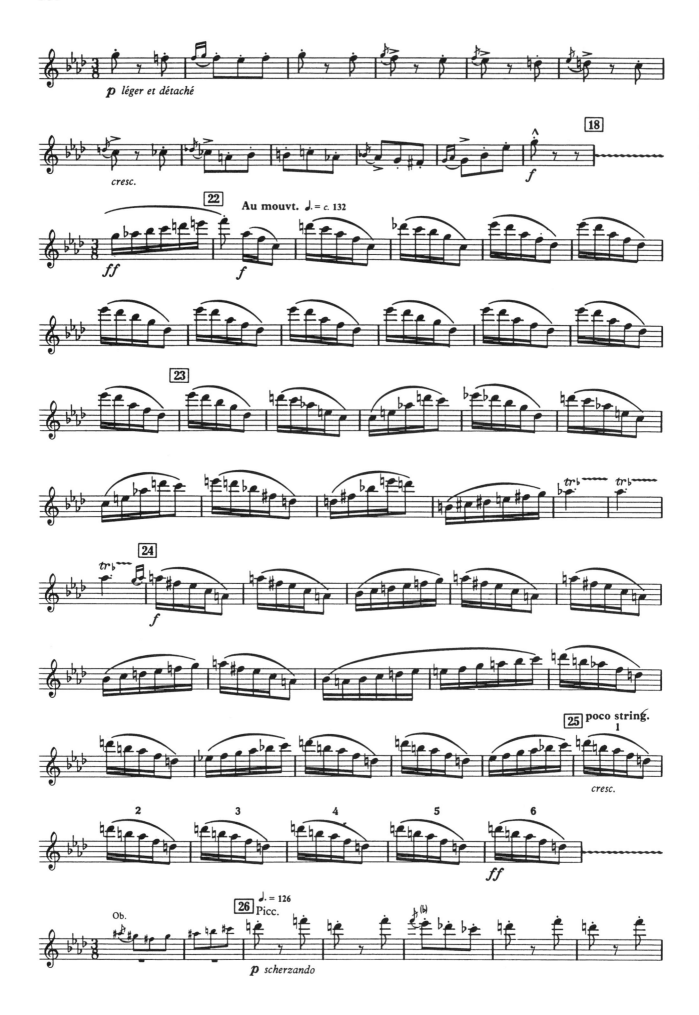

145

CONCERTO FOR PIANO AND WIND
1st Movt.

STRAVINSKY

SYMPHONY No. 1
4th Movt.

SHOSTAKOVICH

THE PLANETS SUITE
I Mars

HOLST

III Mercury, the Winged Messenger

148

IV Jupiter

VI Uranus, the Magician

VIOLIN CONCERTO
1st Movt.

WALTON

2nd Movt.

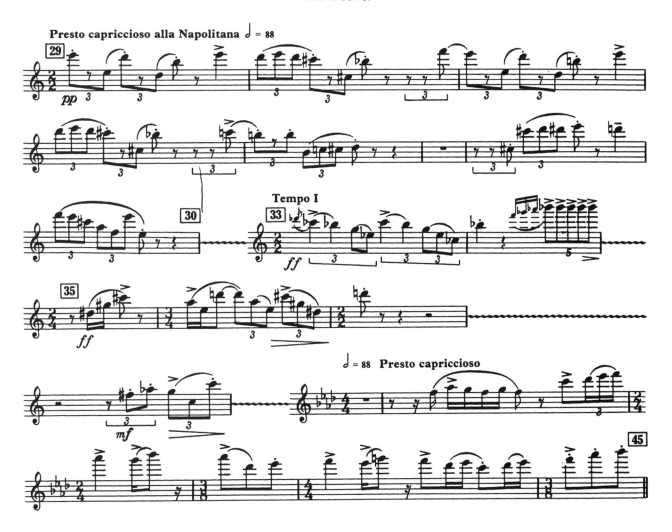

3rd Movt.

FIREWORKS

STRAVINSKY

151

SYMPHONY No. 6
2nd Movt.

SHOSTAKOVICH

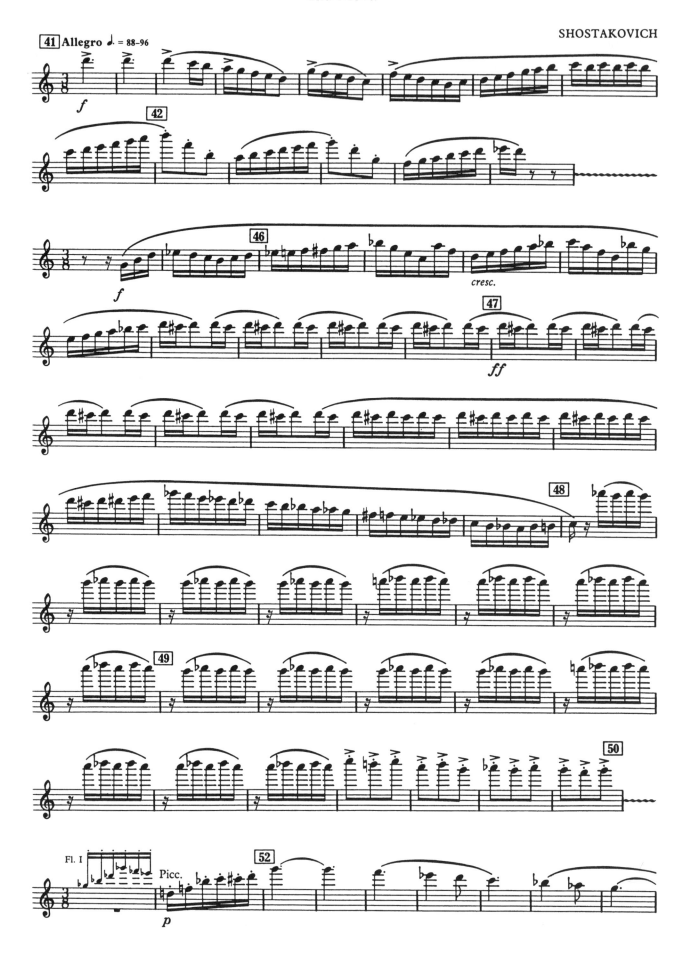

3rd Movt.

154

PETRUSHKA
Part I

STRAVINSKY

SYMPHONY No. 2
(In One Movt.)

SHOSTAKOVICH

PIANO CONCERTO No. 3
1st Movt.

PROKOFIEV

3rd Movt.

HUNGARIAN DANCES
No. 1

BRAHMS

No. 2

No. 3

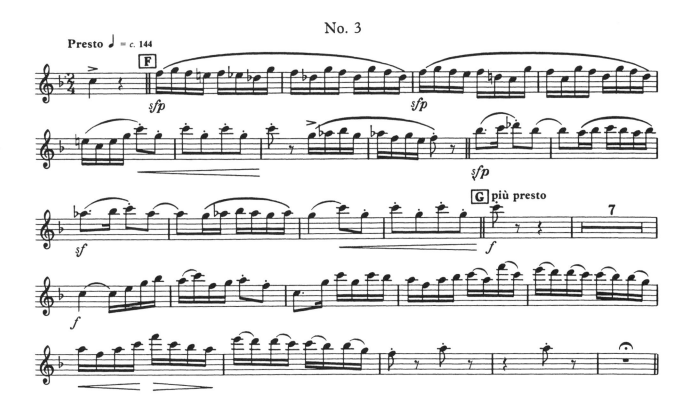

160

No. 18

No. 21

PIANO CONCERTO
1st Movt.

RAVEL

3rd Movt.

SEA INTERLUDES from 'PETER GRIMES'
STORM

BRITTEN

162

SYMPHONY No. 10
1st Movt.

SHOSTAKOVICH

2nd Movt.

164

3rd Movt.

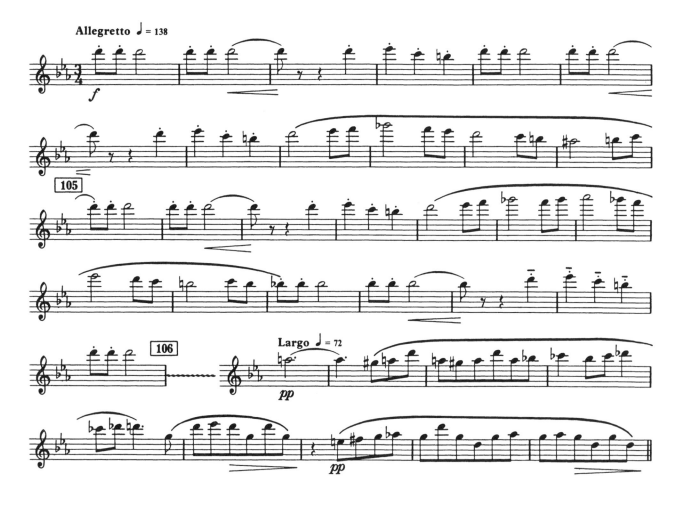

4th Movt.

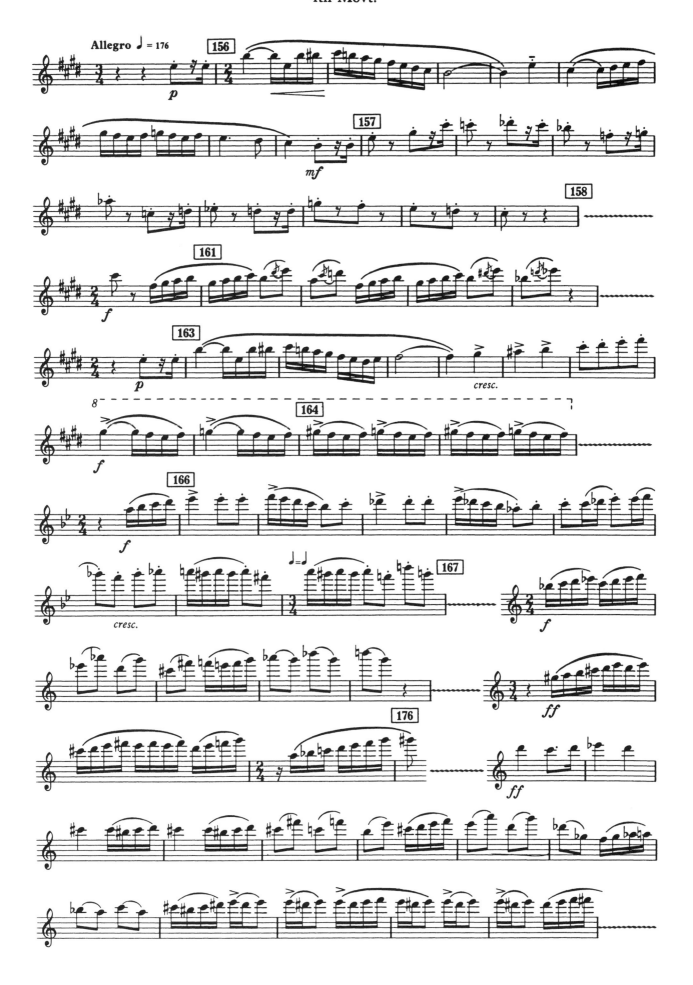

THE MIRACULOUS MANDARIN

BARTÓK

167

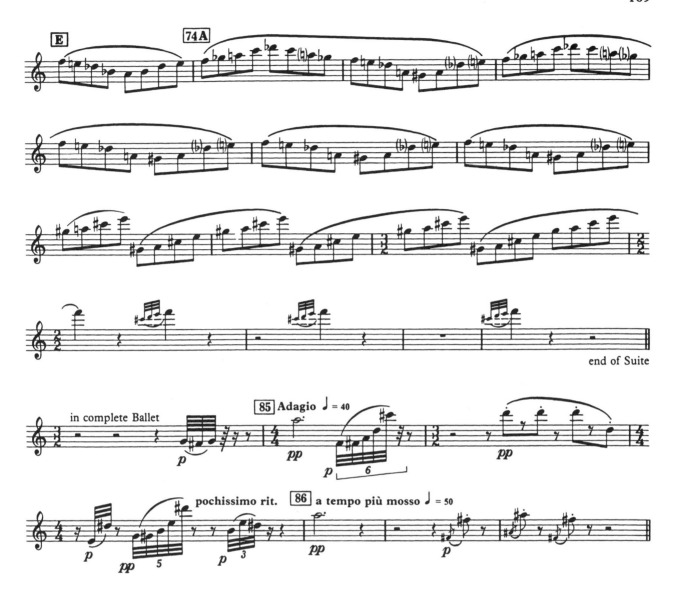

end of Suite

BACCHUS ET ARIANE
2nd Suite

ROUSSEL

LA PERI

DUKAS

172

DON QUIXOTE

R. STRAUSS

Der ritter von der traurigen gestalt

OVERTURE – CARNIVAL

DVOŘÁK

SYMPHONY No. 6
3rd Movt.

TCHAIKOVSKY

DAPHNIS AND CHLÖE

Part I

RAVEL

Part II

SYMPHONY No. 3
1st Movt.

SHOSTAKOVICH

KAMMERMUSIK No. 4
2nd Movt.

HINDEMITH

181

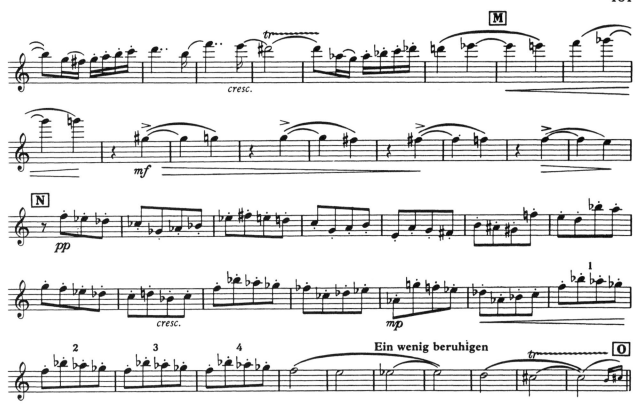

3rd Movt. – Nachtstück

4th Movt.

5th Movt.

SYMPHONY No. 8
Final scene – (2nd section)

MAHLER

THE PINES OF ROME
I pini di Villa Borghese

RESPIGHI

SECTION G
Piccolo Duets

The earlier reference to 'Difference Tones' in Section C – Loud playing – will mean more to you when you practise these orchestral duets with a friend, especially in the second and third octaves. Frequently check your overall tuning either with a tuning machine or a reliable piano.

SYMPHONY No. 10
1st Movt.

SHOSTAKOVICH

MENUET DES FOLLETS

BERLIOZ

188

SLAVONIC MARCH

TCHAIKOVSKY

190

An interesting piece of orchestration here, the horn and celeste are playing this same theme in C major whilst the piccolos are in E and G major. The idea is for the piccolos to play so quietly that they fuse with the horn tone colour!

BOLERO

RAVEL

FOUR SCOTTISH DANCES
No. 4

ARNOLD

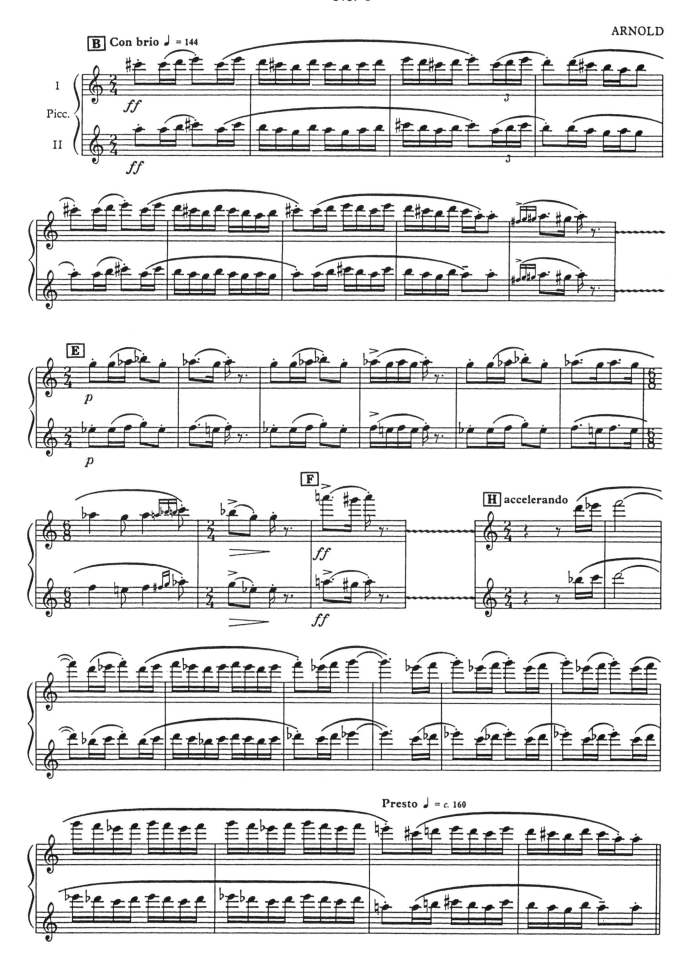

CARMEN SUITE
4th Movt.

BIZET

SECTION H
Coda

A WORK-OUT ROUTINE

After all the serious practice, it's a good idea to use these extracts from the 4th Symphony of Shostakovich as a work-out and to check up on your progress. They contain most of the points covered in this book.

4th SYMPHONY
1st Movt.

SHOSTAKOVICH

ARTICULATION

TOP REGISTER: FINGERS

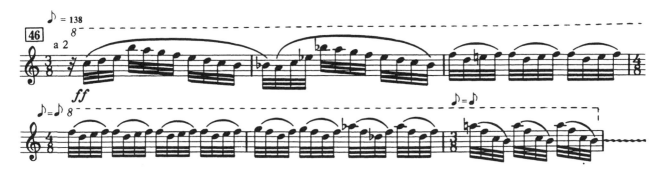

ARTICULATION

2nd Movt.

THE TOP

DUET: SOFT PLAYING

196

FLUTTER TONGUING

LOW REGISTER

3rd Movt.

AUDITIONS

Here is a short list of pieces which are most likely to show up at an orchestral audition. A thorough knowledge of these works would, other things being equal, increase your chances of success.

Very probable audition pieces

BARTÓK	Concerto for Orchestra
	Pe Loc from Roumanian Dances
BEETHOVEN	Symphony Nos. 5 and 9
BERLIOZ	Menuet des Follets
	Symphonie Fantastique
	Overture – *Beatrice and Benedict*
BORODIN	Polotsvian Dances
BRAHMS	Symphony No. 4 – 3rd Movt.
BRITTEN	Young Person's Guide to the Orchestra – *Fugue*
DELIBES	Ballet Music – *Coppelia*
DUKAS	The Sorcerer's Apprentice
GOUNOD	Ballet Music – *Faust*
HOLST	Ballet Suite – *The Perfect Fool*
	Suite – *The Planets*
IPPOLITOV-IVANOV	Caucasian Sketches
KODALY	Dances of Galanta
	Suite – *Hary Janos*
PROKOFIEV	Lieutenant Kije
RAVEL	Piano Concerto in G
	Bolero
	2nd Suite – *Daphnis and Chlöe*
	Suite – *Mother Goose*
RIMSKY-KORSAKOV	Scheherazade
ROSSINI	Overture – *The Thieving Magpie*
	Overture – *Semiramide*
	Overture – *The Silken Ladder*
SHOSTAKOVICH	Symphony Nos. 5, 6, 8, 9, 10
J. STRAUSS	Perpetuum Mobile
R. STRAUSS	Ein Heldenleben
STRAVINSKY	Suite – *The Firebird*
TCHAIKOVSKY	Symphony Nos. 4 and 6

And, of course, the Vivaldi Piccolo Concertos, the only 'real' solos for the piccolo. They are often set as audition solos.

BUYING A PICCOLO

Unless you are familiar with the range of piccolos currently available in the shops, it would be wiser to ask for expert advice on this subject. If you are new to piccolo playing, your teacher should be able to help.

If, however, you are looking for a more serious – and expensive instrument, one of the orchestral Principals in a Symphony Orchestra may be prepared to offer advice.

Broadly there are two kinds of piccolo; metal and wood, and two bore shapes; conical and cylindrical. A cylindrical body has a conical head joint; a conical body has a cylindrical head.

The bore first; a cylindrical piccolo – which is usually made of metal (though not all metal piccolos have a cylindrical bore) – is easier to play throughout the whole range. The third octave is noticeably freer. However, it often suffers from such problems as a thin sound and less variety of tone colour. The conical bore piccolos, on the other hand, are generally more difficult above top A or B flat but usually sound nicer.

There are various plastic compounds, too, and mixtures of wood and metal.

The merits of the various combinations of material are difficult to elucidate; the only real answer is to try them.

Some piccolos have metal heads with plastic lip plates. The lip plates are sometimes of the 'Reform' variety, that is, with 'wings'. Sometimes, the removal, by filing, of these wings, has transformed the whole instrument.

Instruments respond differently to different head pieces, too.

One very nice point about conical bore piccolos is that the head joint is cylindrical and therefore any piece of cylindrical tubing of 11 millimetres in diameter is a potential head joint. Lip plates can easily be formed by bending – in heat – a piece of perspex. Taking any other head as a model, a clean hole should be cut and shaped; the socket end will then have to be fitted in the body of the piccolo. This should be looked at by anyone handy at making things because head joints can be made to suit different purposes, for instance, a shallower mouth hole (a thin lip plate) will make the top notes easier; a deeper one will cause problems at the top end but make the lower octave stronger.

Similarly, undercutting the mouth hole will strengthen the upper partials, making the top register easier; it also changes the overall tone and causes buzziness.

A serious orchestral player would usually have more than one instrument and certainly more than one head piece. It's a wise player who has two or even three head joints to make life easier.

Generally, the one-instrument player would choose a conical bore wooden piccolo. If this is *your* choice, try to take some spare head joints with you for trials when buying. A different head can work wonders.

Here are some pointers:

(a) Practise before you go to the shop so as to be in good form.

(b) Try out all they have – maybe as many as eight or ten different piccolos; put aside three or four which interest you, and if possible, change heads around.

(c) Try it through the whole compass – a lovely middle octave is useless unless the top and bottom are O.K.

(d) Try head joints for (i) rapid articulation, (ii) octaves and general flexibility.

(e) If it's an old piccolo *take a tuning machine*; there are some lovely sounding old piccolos around which are very difficult to play in tune. Piccolos – as flutes – suffer from the change in pitch since the 1930's from A = 435 to A = 440 or 442. It's wise to take a tuning machine anyway!

(f) The condition of springs and pads isn't important (except that these may prevent a proper trial) but do check for worn keywork or amateur do-it-yourself repairs, perhaps done badly.

Some head joints have a cut-away section in the wood just where the air strikes the opposite edge of the hole. The reasons for this sharp edge are that the top end should be freer, and articulation should be brighter.

The market is always changing and the authors have seen good instruments appearing from time to time at a relatively cheap price. You don't *have* to spend a lot of money – the most important thing is to select the piccolo intelligently, and if in doubt, seek advice.

The money you have available is mostly the main factor; keep some of it aside and spend it on a separate head joint.

Finally, good luck with your experiments and we hope that, whether you are masquerading as a soulful 'little flute', or indulging in a fit of megolomania drowning the efforts of your colleagues, you will have fun.

Further Repertoire: Opera and Ballet

We have used the orchestral repertoire and left the opera and ballet repertoire perhaps for a future volume. Some opera and ballet excerpts will appear in the concert repertoire from time to time; should you wish to explore these areas more fully, we would recommend:

ORCHESTER STUDIEN for piccolo by KURT NITSCHKE published by PETERS, Vol. I and II

STUDI DI ORCHESTRA for flute and piccolo by TORCHIO published by RICORDI, Vol. I and II

Piccolo Pieces – Various albums of solos with piano – usually a reduction of a military band or orchestral accompaniment – can sometimes be found amongst second-hand music shops or from libraries. Most of these are long out of print and copyright and so photocopying may be legal . . ! Two volumes of solos have recently been published by BROEKMANS VAN POPPEL of Amsterdam for piccolo and piano and contain the best of the one hundred or more solos originally published at the turn of the century and after. These solos are valuable practice and contain tuneful examples of the main points raised in this book.

Chamber Works containing important piccolo parts are listed here for further reference and include pieces for piccolo and piano:

ARRIGO, Girolama	Fluxus Fl. (Picc.) Cl. Bass Cl. Bsn. Tpt. Hp. Vln. Vla. Cb.	BRUZZICHELLI
DUBENSKY, Arcady	Concerto Picc. and Orchestra	RICORDI
EITLER, Esteban	Divertimento Picc. Cl. Bass Cl. Gtr.	HEUGEL
FIELDS, Frank	Chant Ritual No. 1 Picc. 2 Flts. 2 Obs. 2 Cls. Bass Cl. 2 Bsns. C.Bsn. Timp.	PEER
HALETZKI, Paul	Intermezzo Scherzo Picc. Bsn. Pno.	SCHOTT
HINDEMITH, Paul	Kleine Kammermusik Fl. (Picc.) Ob. Cl. Bsn. Hn.	SCHOTT
HINDEMITH, Paul	'The Demon Concert Suite' from the Ballet *Pantomime* Fl. (Picc.) Cl. Hn. Tpt.	SCHOTT
HONEGGER, Arthur	Trois Contrepoints Picc. Ob. (EH) Vln. Vcl.	HANSEN
HONEGGER, Arthur	Contrepoint No. 1 Picc. Vcl.	HANSEN
HUYBRECHTS, Albert	Sextet Pastorale 2 Fls. (Picc.) Ob. Cl. Bsn. Hn.	CEBEDEM
IVES, Charles	Scherzo 'Over the Pavements' Picc. Cl. Bsn. Tpt. 3 Trbs. Perc. Pno.	PEER
JACOB, Gordon	Trio Fl. (Picc.) Ob. Hpschd. or Pno.	OXFORD UNIVERSITY PRESS
JANÁČEK, Leos	Mladi (Youth) Suite Fl. (Picc.) Ob. Cl. Bass Cl. Bsn. Hn.	ARTIA
KABELAC, Miloslav	Sextet Fl. (Picc.) Ob. (Cl.) Cl.I (Alto Sax.) Cl.II (Bass Cl.) Bsn. Hn.	STATNI HUD. FOND.
KATZ, Erich	Toy Concerto Picc. Celesta Perc.	McGINNIS & MARX
KEIPER, William	Piccolo and Piccola 2 Piccs. and small Orch. (or Pno.)	MELODIE
KRENEK, Ernst	Quintet Fl. (Picc.) Ob. Cl. Bsn. Hn.	BARENREITER
LIADOV, Anatol	Une Tabatiere a Musique (arr. Composer) Picc. 2 Fls. 3 Cls. Hp. Bells	ASSOC. MUSIC
LUTYENS, Elizabeth	Concertante for 5 players Fl. (Picc.) Cl. (Bass Cl.) Vln. (Vla.) Vcl. Pno.	MILLS MUSIC

MAMANGAKIS, Nikos	Konstructionen Fl. (Picc.) Perc. (3 players)	MODERN
MIGNONE, Francisco	Urutan Picc. Fl. Cl. Bsn. Pf. (4 hands)	INST. INT. DE MUS.
MILHAUD, Darius	Printemps (Symphonie 1) Picc. Fl. Ob. Cl. 2 Vlns. Vla. Vcl. Hp.	UNIVERSAL EDITION
MILHAUD, Darius	Symphonie 5 Picc. Fl. Ob. EH Cl. Bass Cl. 2 Bsns. 2 Hns.	UNIVERSAL EDITION
NILSSON, B.	20 Gruppen Picc. Ob. Cl.	UNIVERSAL EDITION
NILSSON, B.	Frequenzen Fl. Picc. Vib. Xyl. Cb. Gtr. Perc. (2 players)	UNIVERSAL EDITION
NILSSON, B.	Zeitem im umlauf Fl. Picc. Ob. EH. Cl. Bass Cl. Ten.Sax. Bsn.	UNIVERSAL EDITION
PALLAGNANS, Angelo	Musica Da Camera Picc. Fl. Bass Cl. Hn. Vib. Hp. Vln. Vcl. Cb.	UNIVERSAL EDITION
PETREK, Felix	Divertimento 2 Fls. (Picc.) Ob. Cl. 2 Bsns. 2 Hns.	ANDRAUD
POPOV, Gabriel	Septet Fl. (Picc.) Cl. Bsn. Tpt. Vln. Vcl. Cb.	UNIVERSAL EDITION
RAXACH, Enrique	Estrofas Fl. (Picc.) Bass Cl. (Cl.) Vln. Vcl. Cb. Perc.	TONOS
REVUELTAS, Silvestre	Little Piece Picc. Ob. Cl. Bar.Sax. Tpt.	PEER
REVUELTAS, Silvestre	Toccata Vln. Picc. E flat Cl. Cl. (Bass Cl.) Hn. Tpt. Timp.	PEER
REYNOLDS, Roger	Wedge 2 Fls. (Picc.) 2 Tpts. 2 Trbs. Tuba Perc. Cb. Pno.	PETERS
RUBBRA, Edmund	Notturno Picc. Fl. Ob. Cl.	LENGNICK
SALMHOFER, Franz	Kammersuite Fl. (Picc.) 2 Obs. Cl. Bass Cl. 2 Bsns. 2 Hns. 2 Vlns. Vla. Vcl. Cb. Hp.	UNIVERSAL EDITION
SANDLOFF, Peter	Fest Der Tiere Fl. (Picc.) Ob. Cl. Bsn.	MODERN
SCHAT, Peter	Improvisations and symphonies Fl. (Picc.) Ob. Cl. Bsn. Hn.	DONEMUS
SCHIBLER, Armin	Kaleidoskop Fl. (Picc.) Ob. Cl. Bsn. Hn.	SIMROCK
SCHÖNBERG, Arnold	Quintet Fl. (Picc.) Ob. Cl. Bsn. Hn.	UNIVERSAL EDITION
SHOSTAKOVICH, D.	3 Waltzes Fl. (Picc.) Cl. Pno.	MUSICA RARA
SCHULOFF, Erwin	Concertino Fl. (Picc.) Vla. Cb.	UNIVERSAL EDITION

STRAVINSKY, Igor	Song of the Hauleurs on the Wolga Picc. Fl. Ob. Cl. Bsn. 2 Hns.	BOOSEY & HAWKES
SZALONEK, W.	Aphorisms '9' Fl. (Picc.) Ob. Tpt. Trb. 2 wdn. Pears Perc. Vln. Vla. Vcl.	McGINNIS & MARX
TOGNI, Camillo	Aubade Fl. (Picc.) Cl. Vib. Hp. Hpschd. Vcl.	ZERBONI
WUORINEN, Charles	Bearbeituneen Uber Das Glogauer Leiderbuch Fl. (Picc.) Cl. (Bass Cl.) Vln. Cb.	McGINNIS & MARX

PICCOLO and PIANO

DUBOIS, Rob	Bewegomgem	DONEMUS
DUBOIS, Pierre Max	La Piccolette	RIDEAU ROUGE-PARIS
EISMA, Will	Affairs II (Picc. Hpschd.)	DONEMUS
JANÁČEK, Leos	La Marche des Gorge Bleues	ARTIA
JONES, Charles	Sonata Piccola (Picc. Hpschd.)	ZALO
KATAYEV, I.	Chinese Dance Picc. (Fl.) Pno.	RUSS ST. MUSICA RARA
KOEPKE, Paul	Popinjay	RUBANK
LOVELOCK, William	Scherzo Waltz	ZALO
PETRASSI, Goffredo	Ala Fl. (Picc.) Hpschd.	ZERBONI
SHOSTAKOVICH, D.	Polka from 'Golden Age'	ED. MUSICUS
TOMASI, Henri	Le Tombeau de Mireille	LEDUC
WALTERS, Harold	Tarantella Festivo	RUBANK
WERNER, J. J.	Nachtstück	G. BILLAUDOT
WILDER, Alec	Sonata Fl. Picc. Alto Fl. (1 player) Pno.	C.F.G. (N.Y.)
WÜSTHOFF, Klaus	Piccolo Waltz	ZIMMERMAN
WYE, T. (Editor)	Two Solo Albums	BROEKMANS VAN POPPEL

SOLO PICCOLO

CALABRO, Louis	3 Pieces	ELKAN
PERSICHETTI, Vincent	Parable	ELKAN

TWO PICCOLOS

LAX, Fred	Twilight Carol Polka	CUND. BETT.

PICCOLO and FLUTE (1 player)

JACOB, Gordon	The Pied Piper	OXFORD UNIVERSITY PRESS
PETYREK, Felix	3 Tanze 2 Fl. (1 doubles Picc.)	UNIVERSAL EDITION

PICCOLO, FLUTE and ALTO FLUTE (1 player)

ADLER, Samuel	Flaunting	PRESSER
BOOREN, Jo van den	Equilibrio	DONEMUS
CARLES, Marc	Anaphores	LEDUC
JUNGK, Klaus	Esquisses Experimentales	PETERS
KOECHLIN, Charles	Stele Funeraire	ESCHIG
MICHEL, Winfried	Deklamation	BARENREITER
MICHEL, Winfried	Multiplikationspiel	BARENREITER
PASQUET, Yves M.	Lames	ED. MUS. TRANS.
PETRASSI, Goffredo	Souffle	ZERBONI
ZANINELLI, Luigi	3 Scenes	ZALO

PICCOLO, FLUTE and BASS FLUTE (1 player)

GLOBOKAR, Vinko	Monolith	PETERS

PICCOLO, FLUTE, ALTO FLUTE and BASS FLUTE (1 player)

OSTENDORF, Jens P.	Seul	SIKORSKI
TAIRA, Yoshihisa	Hierophonie IV	RIDEAU ROUGE-PARIS
YUN, Isang	Etudes	BOTE ET BOCK

For further reading on the piccolo repertoire, we would refer you to:

Flute Repertoire Catalogue	Vester	MUSICA RARA
Flute Literature	Pierreuse	ED. MUS. TRANS.

PICCOLO CONCERTOS

You won't find much in catalogues though there are a few salon pieces with orchestral, or wind band accompaniment but special mention should be made of:

VIVALDI	Concerto in C Picc. Stgs. Cont.	P.78
VIVALDI	Concerto in C Picc. Stgs. Cont.	P.79
VIVALDI	Concerto in A minor Picc. Stgs. Cont.	P.83

These works are all published by various publishers.

COMPOSER	TITLE	PAGE	SECTION
ARNOLD	English Dances – Set I, No. 1	42	A
	English Dances – Set I, No. 3	42	A
	English Dances – Set II, No. 5	42	A
	English Dances – Set II, No. 6	43	A
	English Dances – Set II, No. 7	43	A
	Four Scottish Dances – No. 2	43	A
	Four Scottish Dances – No. 3	43	A
	Four Scottish Dances – No. 4	191	G
BARTÓK	Concerto for Orchestra — 3rd Movt. *Elegia*	37	A
	Concerto for Orchestra – 4th Movt. *Intermezzo interrotto*	37	A
	Concerto for Orchestra – 5th Movt.	38, 136	A, F
	Roumanian Dances – III *Pe Loc*	11	A
	The Miraculous Mandarin	166	F
BEETHOVEN	Overture – *Egmont*	119	E
	Symphony No. 5 – 4th Movt.	13	A
	Symphony No. 9 – Last Movt.	89	C
	Turkish March	22	A
BENJAMIN	North American Square-Dance Suite Introduction	114	E
	No. 1 *Miller's Reel*	114	E
BERG	Wozzeck	130	F
BERLIOZ	Menuet des Follets	186	G
	Overture – *Beatrice and Benedict*	36, 128	A, F
	Overture – *Roman Carnival*	32, 101	A, C
	Symphonie Fantastique – 2nd Movt.	34	A
	Symphonie Fantastique – 5th Movt. *A Witches' Sabbath*	35, 106	A, E
BIZET	Carmen Suite – 1st Movt.	125	E
	Carmen Suite – 4th Movt.	192	G
	Jeux D'Enfants – *Galop*	74	B
	L'Arlesienne Suite I – *Farandole*	79	B
	L'Arlesienne Suite I – *Pastorale*	78	B
BORODIN	Overture – *Prince Igor*	58	B
	Polotsvian Dances	36, 129	A, F
	Symphony No. 2 – 1st Movt.	107	E
	Symphony No. 2 – Finale	107	E
BRAHMS	Hungarian Dances – Nos. 1, 2 & 3	159	F
	Hungarian Dances – Nos. 18 & 21	160	F
	Piano Concerto No. 2 – 1st Movt.	29	A
	Piano Concerto No. 2 – 4th Movt.	29	A
	Requiem – No. 2	29	A
	Requiem – No. 6	29	A
	Serenade – Rondo	30	A
	St Anthony Variations – Var. V	30	A
	St Anthony Variations – Var. VIII	8	A
	Symphony No. 4 – 3rd Movt.	15	A

204

COMPOSER	TITLE	PAGE	SECTION
BRITTEN	Billy Budd – Act II: Scene 3	50	B
	Diversions for the Left Hand – Var. VI		
	Nocturne	31	A
	Diversions for the Left Hand – Var. IXb		'
	Toccata II	67	B
	Sea Interludes from 'Peter Grimes' –		
	Sunday Morning	48	B
	Storm	161	F
	Young Person's Guide to the Orchestra –		
	Fugue	61	B
	Flutes' Variation	105	E
COPLAND	*Billy the Kid* Suite		
	Scene 1a *Street in a frontier Town*	66	B
	The open Prairie	66	B
	extract	60	B
DEBUSSY	Jeux	17	A
	La Mer – II *Jeux de Vagues*	16, 58, 63	A, B
DELIBES	Coppelia – Nos. 2 & 3	83	B
	Coppelia – No. 11 *Musique des Automates*	82	B
DELIUS	La Calinda	76, 121	B, E
DOHNÁNYI	Variations on a Nursery Tune – Var. IV	120	E
DUKAS	La Peri	171	F
	The Sorcerer's Apprentice	49, 143	B, F
DVOŘÁK	Overture – *Carnival*	174	F
	Scherzo Capriccioso	112	E
	Slavonic Dances – No. 1	8	A
	Slavonic Dances – No. 2	39, 48	A, B
	Slavonic Dances – No. 3	40	A
	Symphony No. 3 – 3rd Movt.	108	E
	Symphony No. 6 – 3rd Movt.	17	A
	Symphony No. 9 (from the New World) –		
	1st Movt.	22	A
ELGAR	Enigma Variations – Var. VIII	7	A
GLUCK	Iphigenia in Tauris – Act I Chorus	68	B
GOUNOD	Ballet Music – *Faust* Section C	56	B
	Ballet Music – *Faust* Section D	52	B
	Ballet Music – *Faust* Section G	76	B
HANDEL	Rinaldo – Aria & Cadenza, Scene VI	69	B
HINDEMITH	Horn Concerto – 2nd Movt.	27	A
	Kammermusik No. 4 – 2nd Movt.	180	F
	Kammermusik No. 4 – 3rd Movt.		
	Nachtstück	181	F
	Kammermusik No. 4 – 4th Movt.	182	F
	Kammermusik No. 4 – 5th Movt.	182	F
	Nobilissima Visione – 2nd Movt.		
	March & Pastorale	28, 84	A, C

COMPOSER	TITLE	PAGE	SECTION
HOLST	The Perfect Fool	14	A
	The Planets Suite – I *Mars*	147	F
	The Planets Suite – III *Mercury, the Winged Messenger*	147	F
	The Planets Suite – IV *Jupiter*	148	F
	The Planets Suite – VI *Uranus, the Magician*	148	F
HUMPERDINCK	Overture – *Hansel and Gretel*	104	D
IPPOLITOV-IVANOV	Caucasian Sketches – No. 4 *Cortège of the Sardar*	21	A
JANÁČEK	Sinfonietta – 3rd Movt.	138	F
KODALY	Concerto for Orchestra	100	C
	Dances of Galanta	40, 75	A, B
	Hary Janos Suite – I Prelude *The Fairy Tale begins*	130	F
	II Viennese Musical Clock	99	C
	IV Entrance of the Emperor and his Court	100	C
	Dances of Marosszek	68, 131	B, F
MAHLER	Song of the Earth – 3rd Movt.	24	A
	Song of the Earth – 4th Movt.	25	A
	Song of the Earth – 5th Movt.	26	A
	Song of the Earth – 6th Movt.	26	A
	Symphony No. 1 – 1st Movt.	28	A
	Symphony No. 2 – 3rd Movt.	44	A
	Symphony No. 2 – 4th Movt.	45	A
	Symphony No. 2 – 5th Movt.	45	A
	Symphony No. 4 – 2nd Movt.	49	B
	Symphony No. 7 – 1st Movt.	101	C
	Symphony No. 7 – 2nd Movt.	27	A
	Symphony No. 7 – 5th Movt.	101	C
	Symphony No. 8 – Final Scene (2nd Section)	183	F
MOZART	Overture – *Il Seraglio*	23	A
NICOLAI	Overture – *The Merry Wives of Windsor*	111	E
NIELSEN	Symphony No. 5 – 1st Movt.	133	F
	Symphony No. 5 – 2nd Movt.	133	F
PROKOFIEV	Lieutenant Kije	107	E
	The Love of three Oranges – 2nd Movt.	102	C
	The Love of three Oranges – 3rd Movt. *Marche*	121	E
	Piano Concerto No. 3 – 1st Movt.	158	F
	Piano Concerto No. 3 – 3rd Movt.	158	F
	Violin Concerto No. 1 – 1st Movt.	32	A
	Violin Concerto No. 1 – 2nd Movt.	32	A
	Violin Concerto No. 1 – 3rd Movt.	32	A
RACHMANINOV	Variations on a theme of Paganini – Var. XIII	123	E

COMPOSER	TITLE	PAGE	SECTION
RAVEL	Bolero	190	G
	Daphnis and Chlöe		
	Parts I, II & III	78, 175	B, F
	L'enfant et les Sortileges	46	A
	Mother Goose Suite – 2nd Movt.		
	Petit Poulet	7	A
	Mother Goose Suite – 3rd Movt.		
	Laideronnette Impératrice des Pagodes	16	A
	Mother Goose Suite – 4th Movt.		
	Les entretiens de la Belle et de la Bête	16	A
	Piano Concerto – 1st Movt.	47, 160	B, F
	Piano Concerto – 3rd Movt.	161	F
	Rhapsodie Espagnol – *Malaguena*	91	C
	Rhapsodie Espagnol – *Feria*	70	B
RESPIGHI	The Fountains of Rome –		
	La fontana di Valle Giulia all'alba	26	A
	The Fountains of Rome –		
	La fontana di Villa Medici al Tramonto	27	A
	The Fountains of Rome –		
	La fontana di Trevi al Meriggio	91	C
	The Pines of Rome –		
	I pini di Villa Borghese	184	F
RIMSKY-KORSAKOV	Capriccio Espagnol – III *Alborado*	109	E
	Capriccio Espagnol – IV *Scena e*		
	Canto Gitano	110	E
	Capriccio Espagnol – V *Fandango*		
	Asturiano	110	E
	Le Coq D'or – Introduction	114	E
	Cortège des Noces	64	B
	Scheherazade – 1st Movt.	10	A
	Scheherazade – 2nd Movt.	62, 64	B
	Scheherazade – 3rd Movt.	22	A
	Scheherazade – 4th Movt.	59	B
	Scheherazade – Last Movt.	65	B
ROSSINI	Overture – *The Barber of Seville*	63	B
	Overture – *The Journey to Rheims*	62	B
	Overture – *Semiramide*	72, 106	B, E
	Overture – *The Siege of Corinth*	77	B
	Overture – *The Silken Ladder*	47	B
	Overture – *The Thieving Magpie*	117	E
	Overture – *William Tell*	51, 65, 84	B, C
ROUSSEL	Bacchus et Ariane – 2nd Suite	169	F
SHOSTAKOVICH	Golden Age – 2nd Movt.	66	B
	Piano Concerto No. 2 – 1st Movt.	122	E
	Piano Concerto No. 2 – 3rd Movt.	122	E
	Symphony No. 1 – 2nd Movt.	34	A
	Symphony No. 1 – 4th Movt.	146	F
	Symphony No. 2 (In One Movt.)	156	F
	Symphony No. 3 – 1st Movt.	178	F
	Symphony No. 4 – 1st Movt.		
	(Work-out Routine)	193	H
	Symphony No. 4 – 2nd Movt.		
	(Work-out Routine)	194	H

207

COMPOSER	TITLE	PAGE	SECTION
	Symphony No. 4 – 3rd Movt. (Work-out Routine)	196	H
	Symphony No. 5 – 1st Movt.	19	A
	Symphony No. 5 – 2nd Movt.	85	C
	Symphony No. 5 – 4th Movt.	46, 86	A, C
	Symphony No. 6 – 1st Movt.	19	A
	Symphony No. 6 – 2nd Movt.	152	F
	Symphony No. 6 – 3rd Movt.	153	F
	Symphony No. 7 (Leningrad) – 1st Movt.	124	E
	Symphony No. 8 – 1st Movt.	86	C
	Symphony No. 8 – 2nd Movt.	20, 88	A, C
	Symphony No. 8 – 4th Movt.	19	A
	Symphony No. 8 – 5th Movt.	19	A
	Symphony No. 9 – 1st Movt.	81	B
	Symphony No. 9 – 2nd Movt.	20	A
	Symphony No. 9 – 3rd Movt.	124	E
	Symphony No. 9 – 5th Movt.	125	E
	Symphony No. 10 – 1st Movt.	162, 185	F, G
	Symphony No. 10 – 2nd Movt.	163	F
	Symphony No. 10 – 3rd Movt.	164	F
	Symphony No. 10 – 4th Movt.	165	F
	Symphony No. 11 – 2nd Movt.	92	C
	Symphony No. 11 – 4th Movt.	93	C
	Symphony No. 12 – 1st Movt.	94	C
	Symphony No. 12 – 4th Movt.	94	C
	Symphony No. 13 – 1st Movt.	94	C
	Symphony No. 13 – 2nd Movt.	95	C
	Symphony No. 13 – 5th Movt.	96	C
	Symphony No. 15 – 1st Movt.	81	B
	Symphony No. 15 – 4th Movt.	34, 96	A, C
SIBELIUS	Karelia Suite – III Alla marcia	103	D
SMETANA	Dance of the Comedians	68, 97	B, C
	Furiant	98	C
	Overture – *The Bartered Bride*	96	C
	Polka	98	C
STRAUSS J.	Perpetuum Mobile	118	E
STRAUSS R.	Don Quixote	173	F
	Ein Heldenleben	73	B
	Till Eulenspiegel	143	F
STRAVINSKY	Chant du Rossignol – Adagio	21	A
	Chant du Rossignol – Presto	58, 60	B
	Concerto for Piano and Wind – 1st Movt.	146	F
	The Firebird – Adagio	9	A
	The Firebird – 3rd Movt.	9	A
	The Firebird – *L'oiseau de feu et sa danse*	136	F
	The Firebird Suite – *Variation de l'oiseau de feu*	211	Appendix
	Fireworks	150	F
	Petrushka – Parts I, II & III	155	F
	Rite of Spring – *Adoration of the earth*	12, 139	A, F
	Rite of Spring – *Dance of the adolescents*	139	F
SULLIVAN	Overture – *Di Ballo*	53	B

COMPOSER	TITLE	PAGE	SECTION
TCHAIKOVSKY	Ballet – *The Sleeping Beauty*		
	Canari qui chante	138	F
	Manfred Symphony – 1st Movt.	142	F
	Manfred Symphony – 4th Movt.	142	F
	Slavonic March	189	G
	The Nutcracker Suite – *Chinese Dance*	117	E
	Symphony No. 2 – 1st Movt.	44	A
	Symphony No. 2 – 4th Movt.	7, 73	A, B
	Symphony No. 4 – 3rd Movt.	134	F
	Symphony No. 4 – 4th Movt.	135	F
	Symphony No. 5 – 3rd Movt.	37	A
	Symphony No. 6 – 1st Movt.	52	B
	Symphony No. 6 – 3rd Movt.	52, 174	B, F
VERDI	Aida – Finale	80	B
	Overture – *Sicilian Vespers*	74	B
	Overture – *The Force of Destiny*	51	B
	Requiem – No. 1 *Requiem*	14	A
	Requiem – No. 3 *Offertorio*	55	B
	Requiem – No. 4 *Sanctus*	55	B
	Requiem – No. 6 *Lux aeterna*	56	B
	Requiem – No. 7 *Libera me*	49, 126	B, F
WAGNER	The Valkyrie – Wotan's Farewell and Fire Music	54	B
WALTON	Facade Suite I – 1 *Polka*	114	E
	Facade Suite I – 3 *Swiss Yodelling Song*	115	E
	Facade Suite I – 4 *Tango Pasadoble*	115	E
	Facade Suite I – 5 *Tarantella Sevillana*	115	E
	Overture – *Scapino*	140	F
	Violin Concerto – 1st Movt.	149	F
	Violin Concerto – 2nd Movt.	149	F
	Violin Concerto – 3rd Movt.	150	F
WEBER	Overture – *Abu Hassan*	110	E
WEINBERGER	Schwanda the Bagpiper – Polka & Fugue	38	A
WOLF-FERRARI	Jewels of the Madonna Suite – III *Serenata*	112	E
	Jewels of the Madonna Suite – IV *Danza Napolitana*	113	E

We would like to thank our friends and colleagues of the BBC Music Libraries, especially Nick Heath and John Lindsay. Without their unfailing willingness to delve into their vast stocks of music, we could never have completed this book.

Patricia Morris and Trevor Wye

On the occasion of the first reprint, the opportunity has been taken to correct errors and omissions. The editors are grateful to many colleagues for their help in identifying these.

ACKNOWLEDGEMENTS

Extracts from the following works are reprinted by kind permission of the publishers concerned. (We have endeavoured to trace all copyright holders but will be pleased to rectify any omissions notified to us in future reprints.)

ARNOLD	English Dances – Set I English Dances – Set II	Reproduced by permission of Alfred Lengnick & Co. Ltd.
	Four Scottish Dances	Reproduced by permission of Paterson's Publications Ltd.
BARTÓK	Concerto for Orchestra	Copyright 1946 by Hawkes & Son (London) Ltd.
	Roumanian Dances The Miraculous Mandarin	Reproduced by permission of Universal Edition (London)
BENJAMIN	North American Square- Dance Suite	Copyright 1951 by Hawkes & Son (London) Ltd.
BERG	Wozzeck	Reproduced by permission of Universal Edition (Alfred A. Kalmus Ltd).
BRITTEN	Billy Budd	Copyright 1952 by Hawkes & Son (London) Ltd.
	Diversion for the Left Hand	Copyright 1941 by Boosey & Hawkes Inc.
	Sea Interludes from 'Peter Grimes'	Copyright 1945 by Boosey & Hawkes Music Publishers Ltd.
	Young Person's Guide to the Orchestra	Copyright 1947 by Hawkes & Son (London) Ltd.
COPLAND	Billy the Kid Suite	Copyright 1941 by Aaron Copland Sole Agents: Boosey & Hawkes Inc.
DELIUS	La Calinda	Copyright 1938 by Hawkes & Son (London) Ltd.
DONHÁNYI	Variations on a Nursery Tune	Reproduced by permission of Alfred Lengnick & Co. Ltd. (UK & British Commonwealth) and Richard Schauer (USA & rest of world)
DUKAS	Le Peri The Sorcerer's Apprentice	Reproduced by permission of Editions Durand Paris/ United Music Publishers Ltd.
ELGAR	Enigma Variations	Reproduced by permission of Novello & Co. Ltd.
HINDEMITH	Horn Concerto Kammermusik No. 4 Nobilissima Visione	Reproduced by permission of Schott & Co. Ltd.
HOLST	The Perfect Fool The Planets Suite	Reproduced by permission of Novello & Co. Ltd Copyright 1921 J. Curwen & Sons Ltd. Reproduced by permission G. Schirmer Inc.
JANÁČEK	Sinfonietta	Reproduced by permission of Universal Edition (Alfred A. Kalmus Ltd.)
KODÁLY	Concerto for Orchestra	© 1958 Hawkes & Son (London) Ltd.
	Dances of Galanta Hary Janos Suite Dances of Marosszek	Reproduced by permission of Universal Edition (London)
MAHLER	Symphony No. 8	Reproduced by permission of Universal Edition (London)
PROKOFIEV	Lieutenant Kijé	Copyright 1936 by Edition Russe de Musique Copyright assigned 1947 to Boosey & Hawkes Inc.
	The Love of three Oranges	Copyright 1922 by Edition Gutheil. Copyright assigned 1947 to Boosey & Hawkes Inc.
	Piano Concerto No. 3	Copyright 1923 by Edition Russe de Musique. Copyright assigned 1947 to Boosey & Hawkes Inc.
	Violin Concerto No. 1	Copyright 1921 by Edition Gutheil. Copyright assigned 1947 to Boosey & Hawkes Inc.
RACHMANINOV	Variations on a theme of Paganini	Copyright 1934 Belwin Mills Publishing Corp. USA Reprinted by permission of International Music Publications

THE FIREBIRD SUITE
Variation de l'oiseau de feu

STRAVINSKY

05/13 (187152)

MUSIC FOR FLUTE

TUTORS

WYE, Trevor
A BEGINNER'S BOOK FOR THE FLUTE
A PRACTICE BOOK FOR THE FLUTE:
VOLUME 1 Tone (Cassette also available)
VOLUME 2 Technique
VOLUME 3 Articulation
VOLUME 4 Intonation and vibrato
VOLUME 5 Breathing and scales
VOLUME 6 Advanced Practice
PROPER FLUTE PLAYING

SOLO

ALBUM
ed Trevor Wye
MUSIC FOR SOLO FLUTE
This attractive collection draws together under
one cover 11 major works representing the
fundamental solo flute repertoire, edited in a
clear and practical form.

trans Gordon Saunders
EIGHT TRADITIONAL JAPANESE PIECES
Gordon Saunders has selected and transcribed
these pieces for tenor recorder solo or flute from
the traditional folk music of Japan.

FLUTE AND PIANO

ALBUMS
arr Barrie Carson Turner
CHRISTMAS FUN BOOK
CLASSICAL POPS FUN BOOK
ITALIAN OPERA FUN BOOK
MOZART FUN BOOK
POP CANTATA FUN BOOK
POPULAR CLASSICS FUN BOOK
RAGTIME FUN BOOK
TV THEME FUN BOOK

arr Trevor Wye
A VERY EASY BAROQUE ALBUM, Vols. 1 & 2
A VERY EASY CLASSICAL ALBUM
A VERY EASY ROMANTIC ALBUM
A VERY EASY 20TH CENTURY ALBUM
A FIRST LATIN-AMERICAN FLUTE ALBUM
A SECOND LATIN-AMERICAN FLUTE ALBUM

BENNETT, Richard Rodney
SUMMER MUSIC

COUPERIN, François
arr Trevor Wye
A COUPERIN ALBUM

ELGAR, Edward
arr Trevor Wye
AN ELGAR FLUTE ALBUM

FRASER, Shena
SONATINA

GALWAY, James
THE MAGIC FLUTE OF JAMES GALWAY
SHOWPIECES

HARRIS, Paul
CLOWNS

HURD, Michael
SONATINA

McCABE, John
PORTRAITS

RAMEAU, Jean Philippe
arr Trevor Wye
A RAMEAU ALBUM

REEMAN, John
SIX FOR ONE

SATIE, Erik
arr Trevor Wye
A SATIE FLUTE ALBUM

SCHUBERT, Franz
arr Trevor Wye
THEME AND VARIATIONS D.935 No.3

SCHURMANN, Gerard
SONATINA

VIVALDI, Antonio
arr Trevor Wye
A VIVALDI ALBUM